YOUR BIBLE

EVERY CATHOLIC'S ESSENTIAL COMPANION

NOEL DONNELLY

redemptorist
publications

Introduction
CONTENTS

Introduction
IT'S EVERYBODY'S BIBLE

"It's my ball an' you're not playing!" We may remember hearing something like this from our childhood days. The result was a feeling of being shut out from the game. There was nothing we could do about it. The ball wasn't ours and that was the end of the matter.

For many Catholics it was almost the same with the Bible. We felt it wasn't ours. Maybe it belonged to "the Protestants". Or else it was for priests who had studied it in the seminary. Or it was for academics, and it helped if you knew a bit of **Hebrew**, Greek and Latin. But for ordinary people the Bible was a no-go area. A weekly dose (or doze!) at the Sunday Mass was normally all we got.

Foreign territory

It's easy for us to feel overpowered by the Bible:
"It's too big!"
"It's not my cup of tea, what with its drachmas and its talking snakes!"
"I switch off when I hear its strange names for people and places, not to mention all those family trees with people 'begetting and begatting'."
And some of us still feel as if we are being asked to swallow stories like Jonah and the whale, or about how the walls of Jericho came tumblin' down (as the song puts it). We can politely listen to the Sunday readings and wonder:
"What has that got to do with our world of mobile phones, texting, keyhole surgery and interactive TV?"

The Church's library

There is a lot about the Bible that we already know. We can see the Bible as a library. It is not "a book". It is a collection of books. This library, again as we probably already know, has two big "rooms" in it. One room (on the ground floor) is for the books that Jesus knew, the forty or so books we call the Old Testament. The other room (the upstairs one) contains the twenty-seven books written in the last half of the first century, several years after the death and resurrection of Our Lord.

Our library, as it is laid out for us today, has its catalogue, the place where we go to find the location of a book. So at the front of our Bibles we find the list of the books in the order in which they now appear in the Bible. (There is probably a second catalogue there, too: this is an alphabetical list of the names of all the books, giving the page numbers where we can find each one.)

So far, so good. But what about all the fantastic stories, like the ones we mentioned earlier? Are we supposed to believe all of these as historical events?

Literary forms

It's important to take into account the intentions of the people who wrote the Bible, and to recognise that they used different literary forms. To do this can be a tremendous help to our faith. We learn (from the Church's scholars) that not everything in the Bible is historical observation, pure and simple. There are different kinds of literature (or "literary forms") in this library!

Just think for a moment about the topic of marriage today in our bookshops. You get loads of different kinds of literature on that subject: you get books on wedding etiquette, best wedding jokes, books that tell you about the Church's laws on marriage ("canon law"), romance stories about love and marriage, collections of music for weddings, books of wedding speeches, great weddings of history, and liturgies for weddings. These are all different "literary forms". In a similar fashion, the Bible contains poems and parables, folklore and romances, songs and family trees, prayers and plays, laws and letters, proverbs and prophecy, dreams and Gospels. And it contains some history, too, but history as seen from the point of view of one side! It can be quite liberating for our faith when we begin to appreciate the differing kinds of literature in the Bible. Sometimes we need the help of scholars to guide us here.

Meeting God. The word of God in the words of humans

But we do *not* need the scholars for us to meet God in the scriptures.

In the first part of this section we have been using the Bible as a window:

> **Hebrew:** *the old traditional language of the Jewish scriptures. (The ordinary people in Jesus' time spoke Aramaic, a similar language which they learned during the Assyrian occupation.)*

"looking through" it, seeing it as a library, and so on. But it is also extremely useful to see the Bible as a mirror. A good exercise is to take a small section of it and hold it up to yourself, asking: what is God saying to *me* in this passage? Try taking a bite-sized portion, and reading it several times slowly. Take time to *listen* to the word God is speaking to you through this very poem, or song, or story, or teaching. Repeat it to yourself, surrendering to the word, exploring what God is saying through it to you today in your real-life situation. Then try to respond in prayer to God's word: in thanksgiving, in adoration, in prayers of love or trust or petition. It may help to become very still, relaxing in silent awareness of God's presence: "Be still and know the presence of the Lord." As you come to the end of your time of prayer with this little part of the Bible, you may feel a call to be with God in some situation of brokenness in your neighbourhood or family. "My word… shall not return to me empty" (Isaiah 55:11).

The Bible is *everybody's* ball, and God wants us to join in and enjoy using it in prayer and action.

Your Bible is offered to you in the hope that you, as an enquiring parishioner with adult questions, can value this sacred library more. You can digest its rich fare by tasting the bite-sized portions outlined in each section. Steady, regular meals will be needed, so pace yourself for the feast!

At the end of the book you may want to begin again! But I hope you will have assimilated the basic nutrition offered in the Bible and appreciate more, as an intelligent adult, one of the foundations of our faith. Enjoy the banquet!

HOW DO I?

Lots of people might like to look up Bible references, mull over them, pray over them, but they have forgotten, or have never been told, how to use the Bible in this way. It is really quite easy when we get used to it.

Suppose we want to look up Amos 5:21-24. First of all, what does this mean? It means we need to find the book of Amos, find chapter five in it, and then in this chapter look for verse twenty-one and read up to verse twenty-four. (In the Bible, the numbers in large print are usually the chapter numbers, and those in smaller print are the verse numbers.) So we go to the contents list at the front of our Bible, find the page number for the book of Amos, go to that page and move forward to chapter five. Easy!

But we need to be on the lookout for abbreviations too. We might be asked to refer to "Ex", or "Exod". Well "Ex" marks the spot where the book of Exodus is to be found. In the same way "Gen" or "Gn" is short for "Genesis". "K" or "Kgs" is short for "Kings". Finally, sometimes there are two books that have the same name. In the Old Testament, this is because the whole story would not fit onto one scroll of leather or parchment. So the writers had to use two scrolls, and we find references to 1 Kgs and 2 Kgs. It looks like we're dealing with kilograms! But, of course, these are references to the first book of Kings and the second book of Kings. You'll find a full list of abbreviations on pages 12-13 and 43.

Here are some texts to find and mull over. See if you can find them in your Bible, and then think about what you make of them.

- **Genesis 17:1-8** tells us about the God of Abraham.
- In **Exodus 20:1-24** we hear God speaking to Moses.
- Elijah's great challenge to the priests of Baal (the fertility god) is in **1 Kings 18:16-46**.
- Amos is not noted for his tact! Read about him in **Amos 5:21-24** and **8:4-8**.
- Some of Hosea's lovely story you will find in **Hosea 11:1-4** and **14:2-8**.
- The holiness of God is clearly spelled out in **Isaiah 6:1-7**.
- The personal call of God to each person's heart is seen in **Jeremiah 31:31-34**.
- That God is a God for all peoples is to be found in **Isaiah 45:20-24** and especially in **56:1-7** ("My house shall be called a house of prayer for all peoples").

THE OLD TESTAMENT

A little help...
FINDING YOUR WAY AROUND

It's easy to get lost when we look at the Old Testament. But it helps if we have a map, a broad outline of where things are.

If you were a Jew at the time of Jesus, looking into the tabernacle in your local **synagogue**, you would find the word of God, in the form of sacred scrolls. And the sacred word would fall into three big sections: the Law (or the five books of Moses), the **Prophets** and the Writings (which is all the rest – Psalms, Proverbs, wisdom writings and so on). "All good things come in threes!" is an old saying. So to see the Old Testament in three sections is a good start. You may remember what Jesus said when he appeared to his friends on Easter evening: "Everything written about me in the law of Moses, the prophets, and the psalms must be fulfilled" (Luke 24:44). That's how Jesus saw his Bible – in three big areas.

If we were to look into our tabernacle in church, we would find the Word of God, but in the Blessed Sacrament. But we can also find the word of God in our Bible. So we are expected to treat our Bible with reverence, as a living presence, waiting to nourish us, like the Eucharist. As we try to find our way around this huge resource, we may see in our *modern* Bible's table of contents that it is divided into four, not three, sections. These are:

- the Law (also known as the **Pentateuch**);
- the Historical Books;
- the Wisdom Books;
- and the Prophets.

How did this come about? The word "bible" comes from a plural Greek word, *biblia*, and this literally means "scrolls". These would be the little separate rolls of leather or papyrus on which the ancient writings were made. Occasionally one scroll was too small for a long document. The story of Samuel and the story of the Kings needed two scrolls each. So too did Luke's writing: his Gospel and his Acts of the Apostles are really one great story, but it needed two scrolls. Then, around the second century AD, a new form of word-storage came about: it was called a codex. Instead of stitching sheets together in a long line to make a scroll, they were stitched on top of one another, and our modern book form took shape.

And so all these little scrolls of scripture, which had been written over a period of a thousand years, now could be contained in a larger book. To do this, they had to be put in order. They began with the five blocks of Moses' teaching; this was followed by the story of the people of God, the historical books. Then we needed wise sayings to dip into, to keep us right on life's journey. And, of course, the writings of the prophets were important as challenges to the establishment in favour of the poor "unimportant" little ones of God's people. So the map of the Old Testament in our Bible has four sections: the Law, the Historical Books, the Wisdom Books and the Prophets. The Bible-arrangers put the prophets last, so that they could act as pointers and lead into the story of Jesus.

It is also useful to have in mind a "map of history". The chronological story of God's people can be conveniently broken up into four big blocks:

1. **the story of the patriarchs** (God's dealings with Abraham, Isaac, and Jacob and his twelve sons. The patriarchs would be of little use without their womenfolk, but that's another important story!);
2. **the story of the Exodus** (deliverance from slavery in Egypt) and the conquest of the Promised Land;
3. **the story of the kings and the prophets** (who challenged the power of the kings);
4. and fourthly **the story of exile into Babylon and return.**

Turn the page to read this story.

Synagogue: *the local meeting place for Jewish worship and education. Sacrifices were not offered there but in the Jerusalem Temple.*

Prophet: *a spokesperson for God. Not a fortune-teller but a blunt "forth-teller". Often a severe critic of kings and religious leaders. Books of the Bible are associated with them and their teachings.*

Pentateuch: *the first five books of the Hebrew Bible, the "books of Moses", sometimes also known as the Torah.*

Patriarchs: *the male rulers recorded in the first Hebrew family trees (Abraham, then Isaac, then Jacob).*

THE OLD TESTAMENT STORY

Scientists tell us that in the beginning there was something they call "the Big Bang". This huge explosion of energy started things off in the universe all around us. It seems that it took place about fourteen billion years ago! Before all of this there was God, a God of love. So that God could share this love, the stars and the planets, the earth and the seas, animals and humans were made. But God did not reveal love all at once. It took time. Gradually and gently God unfolded this love… in stages, sharing just as much as we were able to take at a time. The Bible, the *whole* Bible, gives us in human language the story of this unfolding love.

The story of the patriarchs

The Bible story begins in Genesis with the creation stories; Adam and Eve disobey God and are thrown out of the Garden of Eden; their children Cain and Abel fall out, and Cain kills Abel. Other descendants of Adam and Eve displease God, and God sends the Great Flood, saving only Noah and his family. Noah's descendants begin to populate the earth again, but they eventually forget about God and build the tower of Babel as a symbol of their pride. God scatters them across the earth.

God chooses Abraham and Sarah, from whom will come a nation that will worship God. Abraham (a name that means "father of a great people") we know as the first patriarch (a word that means father-ruler). For Abraham, God is the God of his family. Abraham knows that other people believe in a variety of fearful, moody gods, but his faith in the God of *his* family is so strong that he listens to God and travels in obedience to God's call: "Go from your country and your kindred and your father's house to the land that I will show you. I will make of you a great nation."

Abraham is followed by his son Isaac, and then Isaac's son Jacob. It can be a bit confusing to remember all this, especially since Jacob gets a change of name after he wrestles with God! (God renames him "Israel", which means something like "the man who struggles with God".) Israel seems to have been a busy man, for he has twelve sons who, eventually, become

But when were things written down?

The patriarchs were nomadic herdsmen, travelling from place to place with their flocks. We cannot expect them to have been writing things down, even if they knew how to. Family stories were simply and powerfully handed down over the campfires by word of mouth, in what we call "oral tradition".

The story of the Exodus

leaders of the twelve tribes of Israel. One of these sons is Joseph, sold into slavery in Egypt by his jealous brothers. Joseph's brothers move to Egypt in a time of famine. After Joseph's death, the people of Israel become slaves to the Egyptians. They are ruled over by Pharaoh.

Moses is born an Israelite, but raised as Pharaoh's daughter's son. He hears God speaking from the burning bush and subsequently becomes the charismatic leader who leads the Hebrews out of Egyptian slavery, intending to take them to the Promised Land. Pharaoh opposes this, but God sends ten plagues, which the Egyptian people suffer, yet the Israelites are spared. This is the origin of the Jewish feast of Passover, because the final plague literally passes over the Israelites. Moses and the Israelites escape; God parts the Red Sea to help them.

Moses has learned something new about God – that God is a caring and liberating God: "I have observed the misery of my people… I have heard their cry… I have come down to deliver them"; "I will redeem you with an outstretched arm and with mighty acts."

Neither can we expect Hebrew slaves in Egypt to have got involved in writing. Egyptian writing was extremely complicated and only the learned, usually priests and civil servants, were able to read and write. But in due course the Hebrew tribes conquered the Promised Land. A new alphabet had been invented, which did not need pictures for every word. It used the same letters for similar sounds ("consonants").

Kings and prophets

Here is a *reliable* God, not just a family God. The Israelites journey into the wilderness where, at Mount Sinai, Moses is given the Ten Commandments.

The Israelites, however, continually rebel against Moses and God, and it takes a whole generation to pass away before God is ready to lead them out of the wilderness, where they have been for forty years.

Moses dies before the Israelites can enter the Promised Land, and it is Joshua who eventually leads them there. In the Promised Land, the people are ruled over by a succession of leaders known as "judges". The last of the judges is Samuel; and then the Israelites decide they want a king to rule over them, as this will give them political unity and strength. So they get King Saul and then King David, who captures Jerusalem and makes his capital. (Jerusalem is conveniently situated between David's own tribal territory of Judah in the south and the lands of the northern tribes.)

When David had conquered Jerusalem he had a city containing its trained civil servants who could write up the traditions of David's own people. To gain "respectability" in the eyes of other nations, it would have been important to have his traditions, origins, old family trees, famous military episodes and especially the tradition of stories about God written down. Because they used the name "Yahweh" (the name revealed by God to Moses at the burning bush – a name that in the Jewish tradition is so sacred that it should never be spoken aloud, but which some old versions of our Bible translated as "Jehovah") for God, this block of tradition is known as the "J" source.

The Law/ The Torah/ The Pentatench

Genesis (Gen or Gn) · Exodus (Ex or Exod) · Leviticus (Lev or Lv) · Numbers (Num or Nb) · Deuteronomy (Deut or Dt) · Joshua (Josh or Jos) · Judges (Judg or Jg)

Exile to Babylon and return

David, who traditionally is credited with writing many of the Psalms, is eventually succeeded by his son Solomon (to whom, in turn, is traditionally attributed the writing of Proverbs, the Song of Songs and Ecclesiastes). Solomon builds the Temple in Jerusalem, but also builds other temples to his various wives' gods. This displeases God, and so God separates the northern tribes (which are established as their own kingdom, known as Israel), leaving only the tribe of Judah in the south for Solomon to hand on to his son.

The northern tribes, however, are easily led into idolatry, and come to worship the god "Baal". God remains faithful to the people, though, and sends various prophets, such as Elijah, Hosea and Amos, to reform them. But the people don't listen to the prophets and so God sends the Assyrians to conquer the northern kingdom, and some of the people are taken into exile in Assyria. Some refugees from the north flee south to Jerusalem and get to work reforming the folk there, just in case a similar fate should come to Jerusalem.

As the northern tribes broke away from Jerusalem and Judah, so the northerners set about writing up their traditions in the way they were used to telling them. Since they were used to calling God by the name "Elohim", this source of tradition is labelled as the "E" tradition. So we now have two roots of some of our modern Bible.

When the northern refugees arrived in the south following the Assyrian invasion, these reforms were mostly summed up in what we now call the book of Deuteronomy, a word that means "second law". Not surprisingly, this is known as the "D" tradition.

God also sends prophets (principally Isaiah and Jeremiah) to persuade the people of Judah to turn back to God. They don't listen either, and eventually Judah is invaded by Babylon. The people of Judah are exiled to Babylon, where the book of Lamentations is written. These Hebrew exiles are now without Temple or army or territory. And they discover that God is greater than these things, and that God is still with them, continuing to reveal constant love in different ways. The prophet Ezekiel encourages them.

Around five hundred years or so before Jesus, a new power replaces the Assyrians. It is the empire of the Medes and Persians. They seem to have been a more tolerant lot, and the Hebrews are allowed to return home if they want to.

In exile, the Hebrews looked around them at the great liturgies of Babylon, and they learned about the creation stories of the people around them. With the help of their priests they used some of the images and stories they found in Babylon and adapted them to tell the great story of the one God, the God of their Hebrew ancestors, who had delivered them, had punished them for their lack of trust, and who would restore them in due time. This clearer understanding of God, refined by the priests, we now know as the "P" tradition, the fourth of the main sources of the first part of the Bible, the Law (or "Torah" as it is called by the Jewish people).

Ezra and Nehemiah tell how the returning exiles rebuilt the Jerusalem Temple and the city walls. Once again, prophets such as Haggai, Zechariah and Malachi are sent to them.

Between the Old and New Testament periods, some serious political changes come about in the Palestine area. The Persians, who (under their ruler Cyrus) had allowed the Jews to rebuild their Temple in Jerusalem, are eventually overpowered by the Greek ruler Alexander the Great. So for several years the Jews have to put up with Greek culture. One Greek ruler, Antiochus Epiphanes (who ruled from 175 to 164 BC), even erects pagan statues in the Temple's most sacred centre, the Holy of Holies. The Jews revolt, under Judas Maccabeus.

Home rule lasts for a while from 164 BC, until the Romans annex Palestine in 63 BC. So Jesus comes at a time of Roman occupation, being born in the time of the Roman puppet Herod the Great and suffering under Pontius Pilate the military governor.

When the exiles got back to Jerusalem, the priests set about "editing" the various traditions into a fairly continuous narrative. They respected all of the sources that had been handed down to them. They didn't say one was right and another was wrong. So we find them setting down a couple of creation stories, side by side, although they seem totally different on the surface. Out of respect we find the editors repeating things, giving different names for the same thing (Horeb and Sinai for the same mountain, for example), setting out several versions of the commandments, eventually giving us what we now call the Torah, or the Law of Moses (the first five books of our Bible). So if one day you make a good resolution to read the whole of the Bible, don't be at all surprised at the repetitions and different names for the same thing. These early editors have slotted everything together so that we miss nothing!

Eventually, over the years, new writings were added from the prophets and the wisdom teachers, to give us our Old Testament. This is the Bible that Jesus knew.

Historical Books | **Wisdom Writing** | **The Prophets**

(Major) — (Minor)

1 + 2 Chronicles (1 Chron or 1 Chr) · Ezra (Ezr) · Nehemiah (Neh or Ne) · Tobit (Tob or Tb) · Judith (Jdt) · Esther (Est) · 1 + 2 Maccabees (1Macc or 1M) · Job (Jb) · Psalms (Ps) · Proverbs (Prov or Pr) · Ecclesiastes (Eccl or Qo) · Song of Songs (Song or Sg) · Wisdom (Wis or Ws) · Ecclesiasticus (Eccles or Sir or Si) · Isaiah (Isa or Is) · Jeremiah (Jer or Jr) · Lamentations (Lam or Lm) · Baruch (Bar or Ba) · Ezekiel (Ezek or Ezk) · Daniel (Dan or Dn) · Hosea (Hos or Ho) · Joel (Jl) · Amos (Am) · Obadiah (Obad or Ob) · Jonah (Jon) · Micah (Mic or Mi) · Nahum (Nah or Na) · Habakkuk (Hab) · Zephaniah (Zeph or Zp) · Haggai (Hag or Hg) · Zechariah (Zech or Zc) · Malachi (Mal or Ml)

THRACE

Black Sea

Caucasus Mt

LYDIA

ARMENIA

Taurus Mts.

CILICIA

ASSYRIA

Nineveh O

Mediterranean Sea

CYPRUS

Antioch

O Damascus

R. Tigris

O Samaria
O Jerusalem

R. Euphrates

BABY

Babylon O

EGYPT

ARABIA

R. Nile

Red Sea

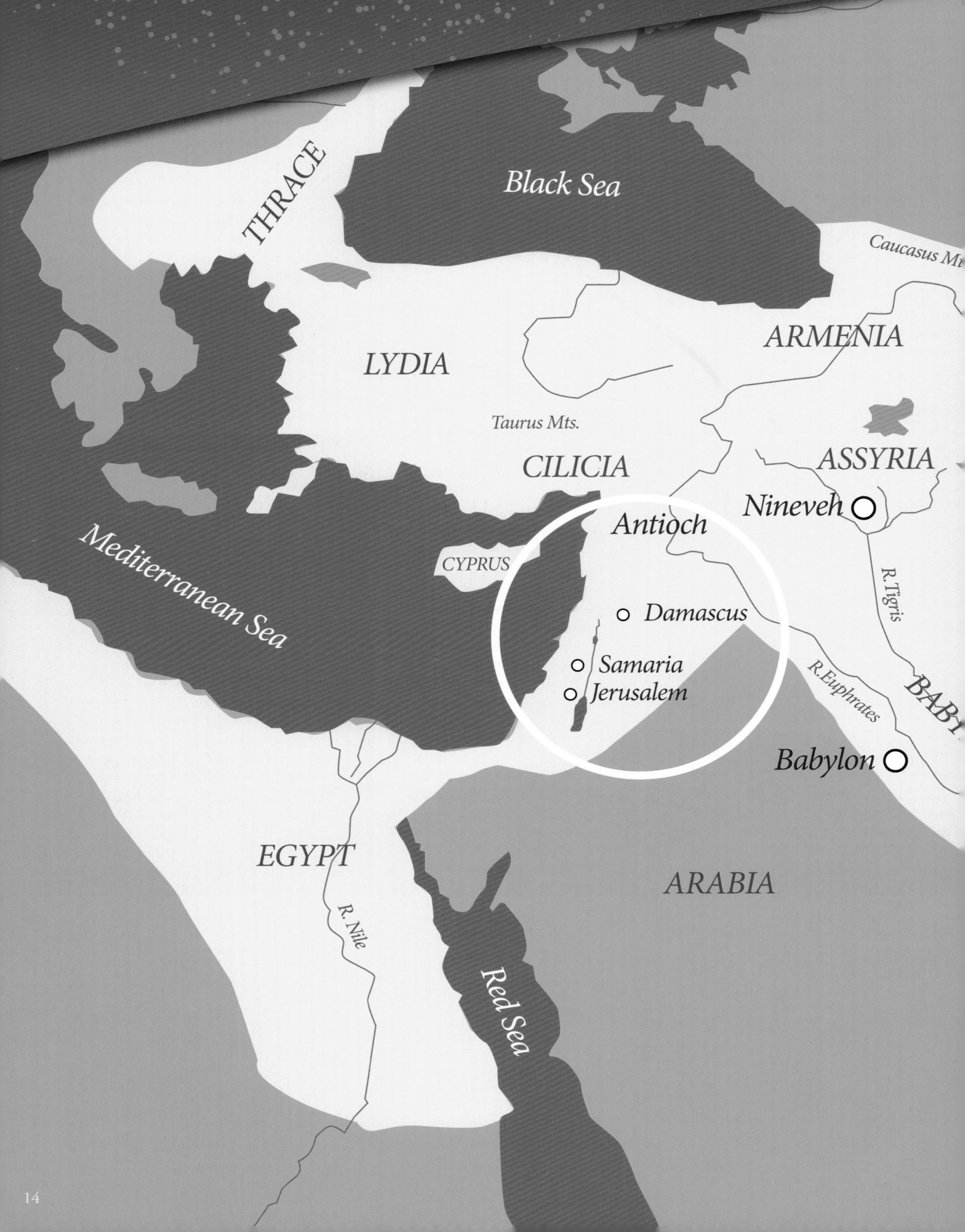

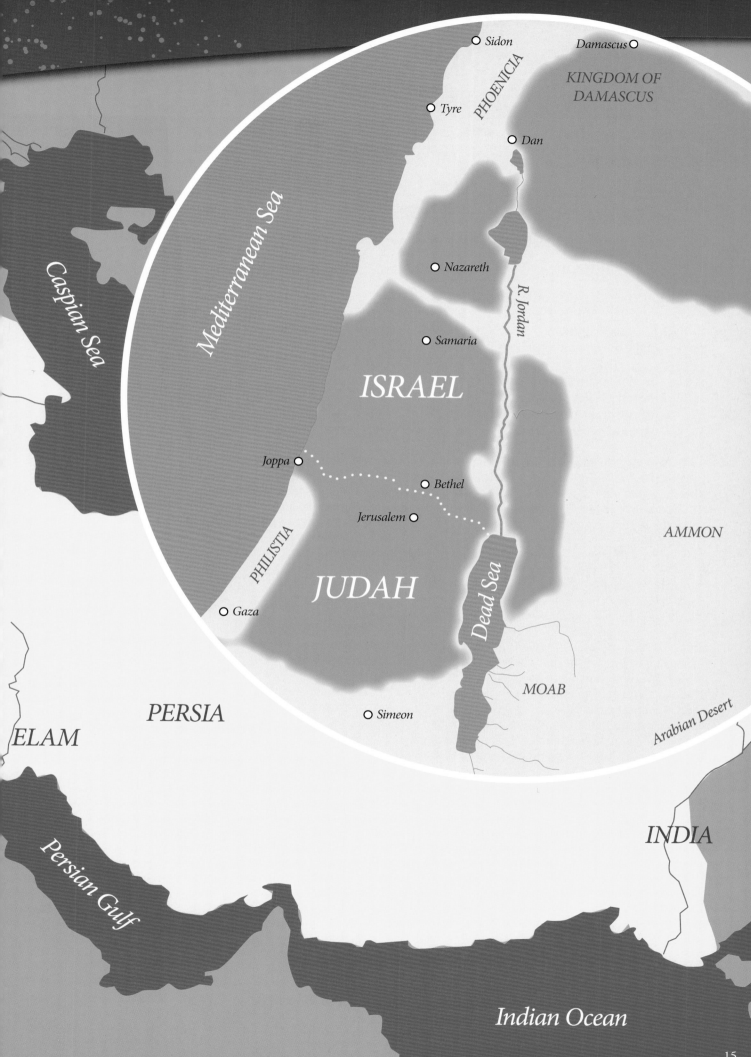

Sidon

Damascus

PHOENICIA

KINGDOM OF
DAMASCUS

Tyre

Dan

Caspian Sea

Mediterranean Sea

Nazareth

R. Jordan

Samaria

ISRAEL

Joppa

Bethel

AMMON

Jerusalem

PHILISTIA

JUDAH

Dead Sea

ELAM

PERSIA

Gaza

Simeon

MOAB

Arabian Desert

Persian Gulf

INDIA

Indian Ocean

Has your picture of God changed since you were very young? Mine has. And as we journey through the Bible, we can see how the picture of God definitely develops.

This is not surprising, since God revealed what God is like to human beings in stages, through people like Abraham, Moses and the prophets, and finally through Jesus.

We have just shared a time-map, showing us the historical stages in the Old Testament. We considered the four broad periods:

1. the story of the patriarchs like Abraham;
2. the story of the Exodus;
3. the story of the kings and the prophets;
4. the story of exile and return.

We make a mistake if we take only one part of this journey and treat it as if it is the finished picture. People often do that. They say, "Look at this! See what God is like!" and they show you some strange story about God slaughtering thousands of foreigners. It's important to remember that we need to consider the *whole* Bible if we are to understand what it's about. Through the course of the Bible we can see how God revealed what God is like *gradually*, in stages, so that humans could take things in, so that they and their society were able to develop in their appreciation of what God was like.

Abraham probably saw God as the God of his family or tribe. He showed great faith in this God as he travelled in obedience across lands where other gods were worshipped. For him, we might say, *God was his mighty tribal God.*

Moses learned that God was not moody, like the gods he had known in Egypt. *His God was a reliable God.* His God would make a "**covenant**" with his people. And Moses knew that, despite the fickleness of the Hebrews under his leadership, God would never abandon them. God's love was constant.

When the people entered the Promised Land with their flocks of animals, they found there a people who knew about growing crops and farming. These people needed rain and fertility, and so their gods were what we might call "nature gods". They had their temples where they "worshipped" using temple prostitutes and this was supposed to help the fertility back home! Hebrew prophets, like Elijah, seriously challenged this: "There is *only one God*. Your fertility god, Baal, is no god!"

When God's people had settled down they became quite lax. Many of them became richer as those who were poor became poorer. The young prophet Amos challenged such people. They were mouthing their pious prayers but thinking about how much profit they could make from oppressing those who were poor. He gave the women a hard time too, upbraiding them at their worship as they dreamed about their menfolk bringing them their next flagon of wine. "No!" said Amos. *God was a God of justice for the poor.*

Then there is the lovely story of Hosea. He was a man who fell in love with a woman who may have been a temple prostitute. No doubt everyone told him what a fool he was. But he loved Gomer, brought her to his home, and she bore him three children. Then disaster for Hosea: she upped and deserted him, heading for the wild life again! Ignoring the "we told you so" jibes of his friends, Hosea set off into the desert to woo her back gently into his home again. And eventually he succeeded. His story is a revelation about God and the Hebrew people. True, they had abandoned God by prostituting themselves with the ways of foreign gods. But, like Hosea, God gently pursued the sinner, perhaps having to send the people into exile to come to their senses, and forgiving them, restoring them to their homeland once more. Amazingly, we have a *God who forgives.*

Covenant: *a solemn sacred relationship, formally entered into, with clear terms (like a treaty) and sealed with some kind of sacrifice.*

With Jeremiah, who saw the power structures crashing all around him during the Babylonian invasion, we learn that God's covenant, or "love-pact", is not a national arrangement. God, said Jeremiah, wants to make a love-pact in the heart of every single person. God is a "person-loving" God. *Each individual is vitally important to God.*

With the prophet Isaiah we learn that our God is a *holy* God. He doesn't just say this once but three times over: "Holy, holy, holy is the Lord of hosts" (6:3). This is the prayer of the seraphs in Isaiah's vision of God's throne in heaven. Isaiah feels this holiness intensely in reaction to his own unworthiness. "Holy" means that God is unique, in a separate class with regard to greatness and goodness. Today we use this triple "holy" from Isaiah's vision at Mass when we join with the heavenly host in the "Holy, holy, holy".

Then, when the people went into exile in Babylon, they were without a king, an army or a temple. Yet God was still with them. God didn't need all these power structures. They looked around and they saw many good people who were not of Hebrew blood. Surely God is a *God for all races*, and one day they too will all come streaming to God and be received in love by God.

For Christians, God is most fully revealed in Jesus. Through his teaching and healing we learn much more about God as Father. Jesus refused to run away from a horrible death by crucifixion, so we can look at the crucified Jesus and say, with the centurion at the cross: "Now I see! That's what God is like!" – *God is totally poured out in unconditional love.* And by seeing him joyfully greeting the disciples in the upper room with "Peace be with you", we begin to appreciate even more the long journey of God's revealing love. The story has taken us from Abraham's family God, through the reliable God of Moses and the prophets, gradually, step by step, right up to the outpouring of God's Holy Spirit at Pentecost.

"Long ago God spoke to our ancestors in many and various ways by the prophets, but in these last days he has spoken to us by a Son" (Hebrews 1:1-2).

The Hebrews are freed from Pharaoh in Egypt (Exodus 1 – 15:21).

We have all probably experienced going through some major event and then, much later, looking back at it in the broader context of life. We distinguish between the event and the later evaluation of that experience. Something similar can be said about the Exodus.

Yes, there was a historical migration of Hebrew slaves from Egypt. But the events of that time were mulled over and eventually written down, with the wisdom of hindsight, many centuries later and in stages.

We have already seen how, around 587 BC, the people of God found themselves exiled in Babylon, a thousand miles or more from Egypt. Here, in modern Iraq, they were powerless in the hands of a mighty nation. Reduced once more to slavery, they wondered if their God was to be relied upon. Was God still with them?

Without Solomon's Temple in Jerusalem as the focus of worship, their sense of community was almost obliterated. Surrounded by new elaborate liturgies to gods they had never known, their faith was seriously challenged. The culture they encountered was based on power.

If they were to retain any sense of identity, they needed to mark out clearly what it was that made them unique as the people of God in exile. They needed to regroup and take stock of their new situation.

A renewed, reinforced sense of identity emerged in this time of exile:

- The sabbath, which had been neglected, was given greater importance.
- A meeting place, or synagogue, for regular prayer and education was established.
- Circumcision became a distinctive physical sign of commitment to God.
- This way of life was shaped by the Ten Commandments.

Without a king, a temple or an army, the people in exile could be identified simply *by their religion*. This is what held them together. This is what gave them their identity and self-esteem under a foreign power.

Above all, their past experience was to be valued. In a complete reappraisal of their memories, during the years in exile they undertook to collect and edit their sacred writings. This effort culminated in the publication of the primary history (Genesis to 2 Kings). At the heart of this memory was *the book of Exodus*.

By reflecting on the events of the Exodus, the Jews now in exile in Babylon realised that they had already been, while in Egypt centuries before, under the power of another mighty nation. They had wandered through the desert for a generation as a homeless people. Back then, under Moses, it had taken a whole generation for the people to establish a new mindset, where:

- the power morality of the Pharaohs was to be replaced by a covenant morality of trusting relationships;
- a reliable God was felt to be in charge, directing their lives;
- community freedom was protected by ten central laws handed down from God;
- and the community could regularly meet for worship in perfect freedom from the Egyptians.

As this had happened before, with God's help it could happen again. So by reflecting on the new experience of exile in Babylon, the scattered Jewish people would learn from their experience – God did not need a land; God did not need a temple; God did not need a powerful army with a king at its head. Instead, God wanted a personal relationship with the people forming God's community!

From this perspective of a people in exile in Babylon several hundred years *after* the events of Egypt, *we* can now read the book of Exodus, with its various layers of "history", as a literary form – the national epic.

In this epic story, the key events are told on a grand scale, so that a scattered people is "re-membered" – put together again as a community. The Exodus story helps to give the exiles a clearer sense of identity, with a sense of humility for past mistakes. At the heart of this new vision is a renewed faith in a God who is reliable through thick and thin.

At the heart of the Exodus story are three key points:

- faith in a *liberating* God;
- God's support in an ongoing battle against paganism;
- God's word publicly proclaimed in ten laws that protect freedom.

Moses challenged the chosen people as well as the Pharaoh… and now he challenges us!

◼ PLAGUES

The book of Exodus tells of a series of plagues that afflicted the Egyptians before the Hebrew people made their escape from slavery. In dealing with the strange accounts of plagues, it is helpful to view them from the viewpoint of the exiled people in Babylon as they struggle with their faith in God.

The plea heard among many of the exiles was "O God, where are you?" Immersed in a culture where many gods were worshipped with great pomp and rich ceremony, their faith in God was in need of encouragement. So the priests helped the people of God reflect on their traditions, especially those that lay at the heart of the Exodus epic.

The ten plagues are set in the form of a great contest between the God of Israel and the gods of Egypt, with each of the plagues representative of an Egyptian god:

The Nile becomes undrinkable like blood: the Nile, the source of life, was worshipped by the people of Egypt as the god Hapi.

Frogs: the frog represented the Egyptian god Heket.

Gnats or lice: these were an insult to Seth, the dog-god, lord of the earth.

Flies: a possible reference to Beelzebub, the lord of the flies. (These plagues would also be seen as an affront to the cleanliness of the Egyptian priesthood, who wore white clothes next to their skin, and who shaved their bodies every day.)

Diseased livestock: cattle and horses were sacred animals, representing the gods Hathor and Apis.

Boils: caused by ashes or soot, used in Egypt to bless, now becoming a curse.

Thunder and hail: Isis and Osiris, the gods of fire and water, are at God's command.

Locusts: the god Serapis should have protected the land, but failed.

Darkness: Ra, the sun-god, is powerless before the God of the Hebrews.

Death: Anubis, the god of the dead, cannot protect the Pharaoh or his heir.

This grand conflict underlines the superiority of God over any of the gods around. What was true for the people of the past can still be true for the present people exiled in Babylon!

It is not important to try to justify the plagues as "natural" occurrences. The authors were not thinking along these lines. They were constructing a "literary form", a national epic, to demonstrate the superiority of God, as a prelude to the grand climax of the Passover deliverance. The ancients did not ask, "Did it happen?" but "What does the story mean?"

All this poses a challenge to our own faith. What are the gods in our modern culture that seek to undermine our faith in God? Can our culture be freed from the slavery of materialism and avarice, pornography, instant self-gratification, ecological pollution, drug-trading, infanticide and abuse, not to mention the great god apathy?

The story involving the Hebrews and Mount Sinai (Ex. 19:1 – 40:38)

It can be absolutely staggering to discover how an ancient idea, known as "covenant", can be so extremely relevant today. People have been bowled over when they've really understood this. Let's explore it together.

Passover

Before Israel came on the scene, nomadic shepherds used to make a ritual feast on the night before they moved from their winter pastures to the summer grazing. They did this each year on the night of the full moon at the spring equinox. This was done in order to placate the god of the territory ahead of them and to call down the blessing of fertility on the flocks.

The shepherd families would slaughter a young lamb, and smear its blood over the entrance to their tents to ward off evil powers. They used this as a visible sign showing the gods that the protection rite had been completed. Then they roasted the animal for a celebratory meal before setting off to fresh pastures.

Genesis 46:32 and 47:3 tell us that the Israelites who lived in Egypt as slaves had once been shepherds. The feast the Hebrew slaves wished to celebrate in the desert, mentioned in Exodus 5:1, may have been a sort of "cultural feast" – rather like New Year's Day: important but not deeply religious!

But God was going to use this human institution in a way that revealed God's saving love for the poor people. The Pharaoh, of course, was only concerned with forced labour for his enormous building projects, some of which were constructed to store his "grain mountains". He had no interest in the springtime rituals of former shepherds.

The uprising of the slaves under Moses, the marking of tent posts with the blood of the lamb and the rules for the annual celebration of the deliverance from Egyptian tyranny are all described in Exodus 11 and 12. These two chapters are central to the Old Testament: it's worth reading them carefully.

Unleavened Bread

Reading these two chapters of Exodus will show up another strand, namely the ritual of the unleavened bread, which much later became stuck on to the shepherd element in the Bible's account of Passover.

The feast of Unleavened Bread was an *agricultural* festival. It belonged to farming populations rather than nomadic shepherds. These farmers, like the shepherds, also had a spring festival. Barley ripened in the spring. The first sheaf was taken to the local shrine, and a ritual offering-cum-festival-meal followed the pilgrimage.

During the seven days of this spring feast, no leaven was added to the new bread – nothing belonging to the old year was allowed to be mixed with this new harvest.

With the passage of time, these two feasts, Passover and Unleavened Bread, became part of the Hebrew culture. Soon they became fused together and were celebrated at the spring equinox. (Fifty days after this feast of the barley harvest there came yet another feast, the celebration of the wheat harvest: "Pentecost" means "fiftieth" and, once they had settled in the Promised Land, this also became an annual pilgrimage feast for the Jews, fifty days after the feast of Passover.)

Covenant

There is much debate among scholars about the origins of the biblical covenant. Some say it is a public relationship with God that is based on an actual event at Sinai; this event is described in the same way that a secular battle-treaty was made in those days. Others say that these covenant traditions bear the marks of later "creative writers", from the times of the monarchy and onwards, writers who embellished and reworked the traditions from their own radically different perspectives. Probably there is much to be said for both positions!

Ancient treaties

I find it useful to think of the origins of covenant rather like the way an ancient treaty was drawn up:

- between two sides;
- in a public way;
- with clearly agreed terms.

A new solemn relationship is drawn up – like a wedding today or a vows ceremony.

Ancient covenants or treaties would have had FIVE parts:

1. The *word* of the covenant (equivalent to the terms of the treaty) was first *proclaimed* to the assembled people. (For example: "Every year for the next seven years, you lot will give me, the great victorious king, one hundred barrels of oil, three hundred labourers for six months, and you will allow me unhindered passage through your territory.")
2. The people were then free to make a *response* to these terms. See Exodus 19:8: "Everything that the Lord has spoken we will do."
3. An animal was killed in *sacrifice*. This was a bloody "visual aid", which starkly implied: "If we break or hinder this word that has just been proclaimed and accepted, then may what has happened to that animal happen to each one of us!"
4. The covenant was then solemnly *sealed* in blood. The people were sprinkled with half of the blood from the sacrifice; the other half was thrown over the altar (symbolising the pagan god, or, for the Hebrews, their liberating God).
    Both parties were now in a new relationship, an agreed communion, "made one" in this one blood. ("Blood" meant "life" for these people – and for Jesus!)
5. The animal was then roasted and the people shared in a communion meal.

Now take your Bible and read Exodus 20:1-17 and 24:3-11, noting the five elements of the Exodus covenant as you come across them:

1. The word or terms of the covenant.
2. The response of the people.
3. The animal sacrifice.
4. The covenant is sealed in sprinkled blood.
5. A communion meal with eating and drinking takes place.

(In the chapters of Exodus between these two passages, detailed regulations from a much later age get mixed up with this story – as you will have noticed.)

In due time, Jesus will announce and become involved with us in a *new* covenant. He will proclaim his own terms or word, summed up in the Beatitudes (Matthew 5:1-12). His followers will be free to make their response. He himself will become the "Lamb" that is sacrificed on the cross.

At Mass we too will be invited to be caught up into this covenant sacrifice meal as we celebrate our Eucharist:

The Table of the Word

The covenant **word** is **proclaimed**.
To which **we respond** in the responsorial psalm.

The Liturgy of the Word

The Table of the Eucharist

The covenant is **sealed** in the **sacrifice** of Jesus.
We acclaim, "Amen!"

The Liturgy of the Eucharist

Communion takes place

The new covenant is celebrated
in a shared meal with Jesus and the community.

Isn't it astonishing how God takes a human idea, covenant, and transforms it into the new covenant relationship with each one of us in the Eucharistic community of the Church? Who said "covenant" was a switch-off word?

To appreciate our treasury of the psalms we need to move rather swiftly from the desert wanderings after the slavery in Egypt. When the Hebrew tribes entered the Promised Land they were ruled by the leaders we call "judges" – men like Joshua, Gideon and Samson, and the famous woman Deborah. But time and again the people drifted away from God and worshipped idols. So God allowed their enemies to defeat them. Each time they cried out to God, and God raised up another judge to lead them and defeat their enemies. Yet whenever a judge died, the people went back to their old ways, worshipping idols.

Eventually, desiring political strength, the people demanded a king to rule over them. So the prophet Samuel anointed Saul as the first king of Israel; and he was followed by the shepherd boy called David. The people now had an extremely astute leader. He conquered Jerusalem, taking it from the Jebusites and setting up his capital city there. Cleverly, David chose a city that had never been the territory of any of the tribes. He brought the sacred ark of the covenant (supposedly containing the tablets of the Ten Commandments) to the city to make Jerusalem the religious centre for the kingdom. Moreover, he used the existing civil servants as his scribes and formal legislators to make Jerusalem the political centre of the new union. His son Solomon succeeded him.

During Solomon's reign, Israel became a rich country. Solomon built a great palace for himself and a magnificent Temple in Jerusalem. However, Solomon also annoyed the people by imposing heavy taxes and using forced labour for his many projects. Trouble was to follow!

The Psalms

As religious life became more centralised, so too were the psalms collected. Many came from the folk-song tradition, while new ones were developed by various writers. We have no idea who actually wrote the psalms, but many of them are attributed to people like King David, Solomon, Asaph and the Sons of Korah.

We can trace four stages in the process of writing and collecting:

1. a psalm is composed (over a campfire or in the Temple);
2. it is linked together with other psalms to form a small collection;
3. several small collections are brought together to form a larger unit;
4. the current book of Psalms emerged, being a "collection of collections", with various individual psalms added by the editors of the final book.

Temple hymn book

This final collected version was the Temple hymn book. It had five main groups of hymns; each block ended with a blessing.

Book One: Psalms 1–41 end with:
"Blessed be the Lord, the God of Israel,
from everlasting to everlasting.
Amen and Amen." (41:13)

Book Two: Psalms 42–72 end with:
"Blessed be the Lord, the God of Israel,
who alone does wondrous things.
Blessed be his glorious name for ever;
may his glory fill the whole earth.
Amen and Amen." (72:18-19)

Book Three: Psalms 73–89 end with:
"Blessed be the Lord for ever.
Amen and Amen." (89:52)

Book Four: Psalms 90–106 end with:
"Blessed be the Lord, the God of Israel,
from everlasting to everlasting.
And let all the people say, 'Amen.'
Praise the Lord!" (106:48)

And finally we have **Book Five: Psalms 107–150**.
The *whole* of Psalm 150 is a great hymn of praise, rounding off the five books.

It was sometime before 400 BC that this was all put together specifically for the Temple liturgy.

The Psalms in the Bible

A final step was when the book of Psalms was included in the third section of the completed Old Testament: the Wisdom Books. (See Luke 24:44, where Jesus refers to "everything written about me in the law of Moses, the prophets, and the psalms".) The psalms too are about Jesus.

With the spread of Judaism over the world, there was no access to the Temple. The focus of community prayer was the synagogue. This is where the scriptures and songs were learned by the often illiterate people. The books were costly and inaccessible, but the responses were learned and sung – and the psalms became a resource for individual private prayer, in addition to their use in the liturgy. The psalms had come back to the people again.

Numbering the Psalms

Shortly before 250 BC, the Hebrew scriptures began to be translated into Greek in a version known as the Septuagint (a word that refers to the number seventy: there was a tradition that seventy scribes were involved in the translation). During the course of this translation some minor changes were made to the numbering of the psalms: the short Psalms 9 and 10 were joined together, as were Psalms 114 and 115. On the other hand the Hebrew versions of Psalms 116 and 147 were divided in two.

The result was a difference in the numbering of the Hebrew and Greek collections: as a general rule, from Psalm 10 to Psalm 147 the numbering of the Hebrew is one higher than the Greek, for example Psalm 57 in Hebrew is Psalm 56 in Greek.

Around the time of the Reformation, the cultural mood was to "get back to the original text", so English translations based on the Hebrew text came into favour in the Reformed tradition.

Today we find the Hebrew numbering system in, for example, the Revised Standard Version, the New Jerusalem Bible, and other Bible translations, as well as in the lectionaries that we use at Mass.

You can check which system your own Bible uses by looking up the popular psalm "The Lord is my shepherd". If it is Psalm 22, then you have the Greek system, the one traditionally used by the Christian Church from its early days. If it is numbered as Psalm 23, then you have a Bible that uses the Hebrew system of numbering.

Hebrew	Septuagint (Greek)
1-8	1-8
9-10	9
11-113	10-112
114-115	113
116	114-115
117-146	116-145
147	146-147
148-150	148-150

The Psalms as Hebrew poetry

This is not a matter of rhyme but of *balance*:

1. A balance of ideas

"When I look at the heavens, the work of your fingers,
the moon and the stars that you have established;
what are human beings that you are mindful of them,
mortals that you care for them?" (8:3-4)

"Make me to know your ways, O Lord;
teach me your paths." (25:4)

"Have mercy on me, O God,
according to your steadfast love;
according to your abundant mercy
blot out my transgressions." (51:1)

2. A balance of stress (metre)

The usual two-line stresses are like:
>   DAH–DAH–DAH
>   DAH–DAH–DAH

"Cry out with joy to the Lord;
serve the Lord with gladness."

A special kind of psalm, a lament, leaves a space for a sob:
>   DAH–DAH–DAH
>   DAH–DAH–(SILENT BEAT)

"From the depths I cry Lord to you;
hear my voice." (Sob!)

The imagery used is quite spectacular; it is always concrete, never abstract:

"You have kept count of my tossings;
put my tears in your bottle." (56:8)

(Imagine yourself coming through the pearly gates and meeting St Peter presenting you with a bottle containing all the tears you have shed in the struggle to get there!)

Or see the stark imagery of a lonely fugitive:

"I am like an owl of the wilderness,
like a little owl of the waste places.
I lie awake;
I am like a lonely bird on the housetop." (102:6-7)

Notice again the use of concrete images rather than abstract ones:

"The righteous flourish like the palm tree,
and grow like a cedar in Lebanon." (92:12)

"For there is no truth in their mouths…
their throats are open graves." (5:9)

"…save me from all my pursuers, and deliver me,
or like a lion they will tear me apart." (7:1-2)

"They have venom like the venom of a serpent,
like the deaf adder that stops its ear." (58:4)

And sometimes the poetic language of the psalms is full of anger. People in those days spoke bluntly to God, expressing their feelings instead of bottling them up: "O God, *do* something about this situation or that evil tyrant!"

"O God, break the teeth in their mouths…
Let them be like the snail that dissolves into slime." (58:6-8)

Psalms today

Over the past few years we've become quite accustomed to singing many of the psalms – and I mean *singing*, not just chanting! It's good to hear in particular so many psalms being sung at Mass: God speaks the word (in our first reading, for example). But God is a God of dialogue: God wants our *response* to the word in the reading, and so we as a community sing our Responsorial Psalm – very often in a popular style of music. (Note that in the Jerusalem Bible translation, the introduction to Psalm 80 tells the choirmaster that it should be sung to the tune "The decrees are lilies", a popular tune that the congregation could use for full participation in the liturgy!)

The psalms are our liturgical songs; they belong to the people of God. They have had a long journey in coming to us. Let us continue to value them.

Scripture and real life
AMOS: A YOUNG PROPHET

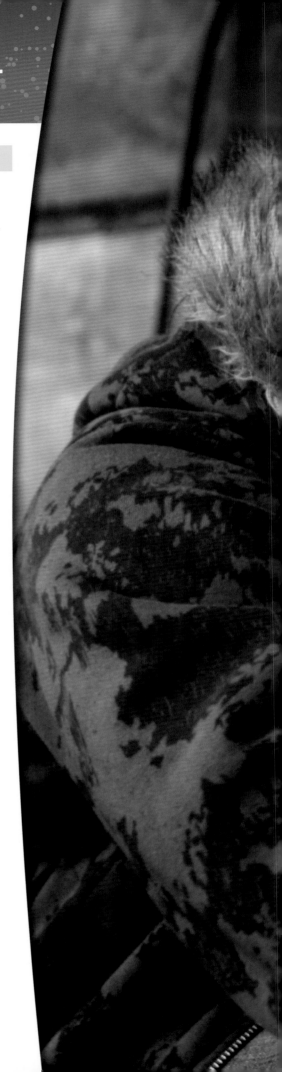

One way of understanding a piece of scripture more easily is to grasp the context in which it was first delivered. Real people were involved.

Take the prophets, for example. We can *read* the Bible section. But we can also try to *hear* it. We can "translate" from the book into real life, imagining the way the prophets delivered their message.

After the Exodus, the tribes entered the Promised Land. In time, David became their leader, followed by King Solomon. After the death of Solomon, there was a split: the country was divided into a northern kingdom – Israel – centred on Samaria; and a southern kingdom – Judah – with Jerusalem as its capital. Amos challenged the abuses in the north.

Reading Amos in context

By the time of the northern king Jeroboam II, around 750 BC, the kingdom of Israel was so prosperous that it acted as if it had no need of God.

This is where the young prophet Amos comes in. He comes north to Samaria, looks around at the worship, and, like many a young person today, he is dismayed at the gap between faith and life that he finds in the worshipping community.

So he decides to do something about it. He speaks out for God.

Amos is concerned with the apathy and injustices that he sees around him. He attacks what we today would call "structural sin" – the unjust structures that result in poor housing and the meagre existence of the homeless people on our city streets; bribery and corruption surrounding the law and politics; the abuse of privileges.

Today he would be questioning cutbacks in social and educational provision, challenging our consciences about the growing gap between the indifferent rich and the hungry poor.

On the constructive side, Amos would be urging further action on improving the minimum wage, on prison reform, on the positive care of asylum seekers and refugees, on the provision of better community centres, and on providing more medical and social support for elderly people and for those with blood-borne viruses like HIV and hepatitis C.

He would encourage those who support fair trade, and the organisations that get engaged in the margins of society like the St Vincent de Paul Society, SPUC and the Legion of Mary. He especially would encourage those who try to get at the roots of injustice by working to change unjust structures: justice and peace groups, and international organisations like CAFOD and SCIAF.

Acknowledging personal sin is important, of course, but surely not at the expense of ignoring structural sin.

If you're not able to read the whole of the book of Amos, then try reflecting prayerfully and practically on the following passages: 2:6-8; 4:1-2; 5:11-13; 5:21-24; 6:4-7; 8:4-6.

Enjoy the young prophet… and we could all listen more to the young prophets of today!

AMOS' MESSAGE

Here is Amos' message in the way he may well have delivered it. It was and remains pretty shocking. As a young prophet, he didn't mince his words when he spoke out to the religious assembly of his day. As a result the priest in charge, Amaziah, expelled him from the sacred shrine.

"Will you northerners all shut up and listen! I don't know why I bother! You are all too set in your ways already!

"I know I'm only twenty years old. I know you see me just as a young shepherd from down south. But I saw you all in the sanctuary yesterday. And I told you then what I thought of you.

"Here was I, feeling I would give organised religion another chance. I went into your sanctuary hoping to pray with you, and all I saw and heard just made me mad.

"You had come from your posh houses with luxurious couches and ivory decorations. Many of you even had two houses, one for the summer and one for the winter. I saw you all singing your hymns, but I could see that your thoughts were miles away.

"You menfolk were thinking about how you could get more money out of poor people. You were quite used to selling poor men into slavery because they couldn't repay their debts. They couldn't even pay the interest on these debts! You use the profits you have made from them to get drunk, and you make sex another one of your gods.

"I lost my rag and shouted out then and there: 'I hate your religious festivals! I cannot stand them. You bring to God your respectable offerings of grain and roast lamb, which incidentally you have obtained by unjust trading. But your religious festivals are just empty superstition! You also worship the star gods, looking for your horoscope! You persecute poor people and give bribes to corrupt the judges in supporting your privileges. Keeping quiet about injustice is now the clever thing to do!'

"And when, at the service, I saw all you womenfolk up there in the balcony, I remember shouting at you and calling you a bunch of fat cows! I said you had just come from lying on your luxurious couches, feasting on lamb and veal, drinking wine by the bowlful, and using the finest perfumes you could buy with the money you took from poor people.

"You like to listen to holy songs and hear them played on the harp. Get real, will you? Open your eyes! See a little bit beyond your own comfortable little world!

"All this mindless luxury and these bribes you give to hold on to your wealth are just crazy. You say, 'I'm all right, Jack!' or 'That's not my problem!'

"Can't you see what's happening all around you? You are so concerned about your own comforts, and the phoney religion you profess, that you ignore the poor all around you. This simply cannot last.

"The society you create is surely about to crumble, but you are too blind to see it. You will learn your lesson when the Assyrians come and take you by surprise. They will lead you off into exile, tying you up with hooks like a string of dying fish. Well, don't say I didn't warn you!"

"I say! I say! I say! Who's the most quoted prophet in the parish hymn book?" "I don't know. Who is the most quoted prophet in the hymn book?" "Well, I say Isaiah! Over 150 times!" "You don't say-ah!"

Most of us are familiar with songs like "God's Spirit is in my heart… He sent me to give the Good News to the poor", "Do not be afraid, for I have redeemed you", "I, the Lord of sea and sky… Here I am, Lord" and many others. Handel's great oratorio, *The Messiah*, is full of texts from Isaiah like "Comfort ye" and "O thou that tellest good tidings to Zion". And at every Mass we join with all the angels and saints in their heavenly liturgy as we sing the words of Isaiah 6:3, "Holy, holy, holy is the Lord of hosts".

Two special seasons in the Church's year highlight Isaiah: Passiontide, when we proclaim what are known as the "Songs of the Suffering Servant"; and also Advent, when the encouraging promises of peace and salvation are proclaimed in our communities.

The name "Isaiah" means "God saves", which is well suited to the message of this great prophet. The man was known in tradition as a family man, a counsellor of kings, a wise and foreseeing spokesperson of God, who, like St Thomas More in the days of King Henry VIII, stood up to royalty and challenged the political shenanigans of his day. His teaching continued for centuries after his death. (Some say he was martyred by being put inside a hollow tree and sawn in half.)

The book of the prophet

What we now have in our Bible, the book of Isaiah, is really a text that covers several hundred years of history and contains material written in the spirit of Isaiah over many years. A number of writers contributed to our present text, though the prophet Isaiah himself is said to be responsible for most of chapters 1 to 39.

In addition to the differing historical periods covered, scholars can detect differences in vocabulary and style over the sixty-six chapters of the book. Moreover, as the book progresses there appear developing understandings of how God works: the first thirty-nine chapters, mainly from the prophet Isaiah himself in the late eighth century BC, are threatening – they proclaim the fall of the nation because of its infidelity.

But in chapter 40 the mood and the historical scene have changed to one of great consolation after the destruction of Jerusalem and during exile in Babylon. A time of restoration is at hand. In exile in Babylon, people begin to see that there are good non-Jews! There is a dawning appreciation of God's outreach in universal love towards non-Jews in the **Gentile** nations.

The unknown writer of chapters 40 to 55 is often called "Second Isaiah". Four great passages here, the "Songs of the Suffering Servant", sing about a suffering leader who will take on himself the sins of the nation and put things right again in the people's relationship with God. Some say that the unknown "servant" here may have been this Second Isaiah himself, who produced at least the first three songs, with the fourth being written about him after his death. Christian preaching saw him

Gentiles: *people who were not Jews (not circumcised).*

as preparing the way for the perfect servant of God, Jesus: Matthew's Gospel, quoting Isaiah 42, says of Jesus,

"Here is my servant, whom I have chosen, my beloved, with whom my soul is well pleased. I will put my Spirit upon him, and he will proclaim justice to the Gentiles. He will not wrangle or cry aloud, nor will anyone hear his voice in the streets. He will not break a bruised reed or quench a smouldering wick until he brings justice to victory. And in his name the Gentiles will hope" (Matthew 12:18-21).

The third section of the book of Isaiah, chapters 56 to 66, is mainly concerned with the restoration after the exile to Babylon. This "Third Isaiah" sees God the Lord as a mother who will comfort her children (66:11-13). The text speaks about the rebuilding of the Temple in 520 BC, though the whole section seems to be a gathering of texts from earlier times as well. It ends with "I am coming to gather all nations and tongues" (66:18). There is a great promise that the Lord is even now preparing "the new heavens and the new earth" so that God's people will live for ever (66:22).

Such is also the flavour of the texts from Isaiah that appear in our Advent liturgy: a promise of a leader who will hammer swords into ploughshares, when there will be no more training for war. We hear proclamation of one on whom the spirit of the Lord is resting, a spirit of wisdom and understanding, counsel and knowledge and the fear of the Lord. The wolf will live with the lamb, and the panther will lie down with the young goat. The eyes of blind people will be opened and the ears of deaf people unstopped. Courage! Do not be afraid! Your saviour is coming! And his name is Emmanuel, God-with-us.

A prophet for today

Isaiah is still calling these days. Is anyone out there listening?

Where are today's servants of God who will stand up in the face of violence and injustice, who will bring Good News to the unhearing and unseeing leaders who promote consumerism, who defend their financial interests in oil and earth's resources through unfair trade barriers and with the remote technology of modern armaments in God's name? "Let there be peace on earth, and let it begin with me," says the song. "Don't let it happen: make it happen!" says Isaiah. (See 58:5-8.)

JOB: WHY DO THE INNOCENT SUFFER?

The book of Job can be seen as a play — a drama, perhaps reflecting on the difficult time of exile. It probes how to go on living when one is deeply touched by evil circumstances.

How do we react in the face of so much innocent suffering? Where is God in it all? Perhaps we could explore the Wisdom writings of the ancient scriptures and see how they tried to make sense of the problem.

An important question in the book of Job is this: can we honour God without there being any carrot or stick in God's hand? Can our devotion to God still go on steadily without regard for reward or punishment? That would be pure worship, perhaps too high an ideal, but well worth thinking about in these days when so many innocent people are suffering.

The drama about Job in the Bible's Wisdom section is well known. Job is a good, honest and wealthy family man who loses everything and ends up scratching himself on a dung heap. At one stage in the story a messenger comes to Job with distressing news:

"Your sons and daughters were eating and drinking wine in their eldest brother's house, and suddenly a great wind came across the desert, struck the four corners of the house, and it fell on the young people, and they are dead; I alone have escaped to tell you.'

"Then Job arose, tore his robe, shaved his head, and fell on the ground and worshipped. He said, 'Naked I came from my mother's womb, and naked shall I return there; the Lord gave, and the Lord has taken away; blessed be the name of the Lord.'

"In all of this Job did not sin or charge God with wrongdoing." (1:18-22)

Job's spiritual devotion is not quenched… yet!

So-called "comforters" then try to explain to Job why he is undergoing calamity and personal loss. Job speaks:

"I am a laughing-stock to my friends;
I, who called upon God and he answered me,
a just and blameless man, I am a laughing-stock…
My face is red with weeping,
and deep darkness is on my eyelids,
though there is no violence in my hands,
and my prayer is pure…
My bones cling to my skin and to my flesh,
and I have escaped by the skin of my teeth.
Have pity on me, have pity on me, O you my friends, for the hand of God has touched me!"
(12:4; 16:16-17; 19:20-21)

The writer takes us through the gamut of responses to innocent suffering:

* this is just punishment for sin (even hidden sin);
* the discipline is good for us;
* God is just testing us to see how we react;
* it may be tough now but it will be fine in the end (the "carrot" argument);
* it is a way of bringing about redemption (of ourselves and others);
* the experience of suffering gives us time to think about God.

This is all far too academic for Job!

The real question arises from Job's tormented mind: "What am I to do while I am suffering?" He can no longer simply accept what is happening. He bursts out into fierce anger addressed to God:

"Therefore I will not restrain my mouth;
I will speak in the anguish of my spirit;
I will complain in the bitterness of my soul…
When I say, 'My bed will comfort me,
my couch will ease my complaint',
then you scare me with dreams
and terrify me with visions,
so that I would choose strangling
and death rather than this body.
I loathe my life; I would not live for ever.
Let me alone, for my days are a breath.
What are human beings, that you make so much of them,
that you set your mind on them,
visit them every morning,
test them every moment?
Will you not look away from me for a while,
let me alone until I swallow my spittle?
If I sin, what do I do to you, you watcher of humanity?
Why have you made me your target?
Why have I become a burden to you?" (7:11-20)

It is okay to rail against God. Even St Teresa of Avila used to say, "O God, if this is how you treat your friends, it is no wonder you have so few!"

The book of Job says clearly that suffering does happen to good, innocent people. As Christians, we know that Jesus himself became immersed in this unsteady, evolving world, with its famines, floods and earthquakes, and, in the face of innocent suffering, was known to complain, "My God, my God, *why*…?" There is no easy answer. Perhaps we are able to hope that God is immersed in the middle of this mess – a crucified, co-suffering presence that does not intervene at every painful upheaval, but honours our dignity by entrusting his compassion to each

one of us so that we may do something practical.

And so we return to the Big Question: *What do I do* during innocent suffering? Not "just accept" but "do", reaching out to others, not with empty feelings of compassion, or still less with academic words of comfort, but acting in practical ways, while hanging on in there to God, hoping with a faith and love not based on carrots and sticks but on the ringing words of Job:

"For I know that my Redeemer lives,
and that at the last he will stand upon the earth;
and after my skin has been thus destroyed,
then in my flesh I shall see God." (19:25)

WOMEN OF THE HEBREW BIBLE

There's the old saying that behind every famous man there is an infamous woman! Or perhaps we should say a less-publicised woman! There are four "irregular" women in the family tree of Jesus that Matthew's Gospel gives us: Tamar (1:3); Rahab (1:5); Ruth (1:5); and Bathsheba, who is mentioned simply as "the wife of Uriah" (1:6). Perhaps now it would be valuable to reflect upon some of the truly great women in the Old Testament.

Shiphrah and Puah
Exodus 1:15-22
Egyptian midwives to the Hebrew women, women of courage, resourceful in disobeying the orders of Pharaoh, choosing life instead of infanticide. Pray for us and for all who choose life.

Bilhah and Zilpah
Genesis 30:3-13
Maidservants to Rachel and Leah, servants and pawns to Jacob in the struggle for sons, powerless and seemingly insignificant, yet mothers of one-third of the tribes of Israel. Pray for us and for all who suffer through misuse of power.

Rachel
Genesis 29:9-31; 30:1-24; 31:14-35; 35:16-20
Sister to Leah and wife of Jacob, suffering barrenness for many years then dying in childbirth. Pray with us in support of all parents who experience difficulty in bringing up children. We remember those families who are getting on with life after the death of their mother.

Dan   Naphtali   Gad   Asher

Asenath

Ephraim   Manasseh   Joseph   Benjamin

Gershon   Kohath   Merai

Miriam
Numbers 12:1-16; Exodus 15:20-21
Sister of the great leader, go-between in the act of saving Moses, yet the one who later challenged the authoritarianism in Moses. Pray for us and all who work for collaboration in ministry.

Aaron   Moses

Amram

Zipporah
Exodus 2:15-22; 4:19-20. 24-26
Wife of Moses, woman of clear judgement and independent action, saviour of Moses, setting aside the patriarchal monopoly of the ritual for circumcision when circumstances required this. Pray for us and for all who take risks for the community.

Jochebed
Exodus 2:1-10
Mother of Moses, inventive in your defiance of unjust laws, saviour of Moses and bridge-builder with Egyptian women. Pray for us and for all who challenge injustice with resourcefulness.

Hearon

Amminadab   Ram

Nahshon

Salmon   Boaz   Obed

Jesse

Rahab
Joshua 2:1-21; 6:20-25
Canaanite woman, sheltering the spies of Israel in her brothel, playing a key role in the entry of the Israelites into the Promised Land, mother of Boaz and great-great-grandmother of King David. Pray for us and for all who shelter strangers.

Orpah, Naomi and Ruth
Ruth
Widows, loyal to one another in your grief, persistent in your struggle for recognition of your womanly dignity. Pray for us and for all who work together for human values.

King David

King Saul

Samuel

Bathsheba
2 Samuel 11:1-27; 12:1-24; 1 Kings 1:11-34; 2:12-25
Beautiful wife of Uriah, victim of King David's lust, power and self-gratification, mother of King Solomon, seen only in the stories of the powerful men around you, pray for us and for all who are caught up in the web of power politics.

One way of doing this would be to find out about their stories by looking up a list of references. For readers who like this approach, such lists are provided. But that involves "knowing about" rather than "knowing" a person.

An atheist can know a lot about Jesus without knowing him and relating to him as a real person. On the other hand, someone who engages in prayer with Jesus gets to know him in a quite different way.

So let's attempt to get to know these women better through prayer. Let's presume that in God's mercy they are now in heaven and so can help us in our prayer. So here goes – but you might like to take what follows slowly, making links with your own circumstances while getting to know these women better.

Abraham

Isaac

Sarah
Genesis 12:4-5. 10-20; 17:15-22; 18:1-15; 21:1-8
Wife and saviour of Abraham and mother of Isaac, traded by your husband for your beauty to other men, yet faithful to God and blessed by God as mother of the promise! In God's plan you became the primary ancestress of the Jewish people and of Christians and Muslims as well. You were known for your laughter and hospitality. Pray with us that people of all religions may treat one another with joyful respect and welcoming hospitality.

Hagar
Genesis 16:1-16; 21:9-21
Slave and surrogate mother, yet the first to be visited by an angel, called by your personal name by a compassionate God; you in turn named God as "the one who sees all". Pray for us to trust in God's care.

Leah
Genesis 29:9-31; 30:1-24; 31:14-35; 35:16-20
Unloved wife of Jacob, yet biological mother to six of Israel's tribes. Your son Judah was ancestor to David and thus to Jesus. Pray for us and for all who struggle in experiences of rejection.

Rebekah
Genesis 24:10-33; 24:59-67; 25:19-26; 26:6-11; 27:5-13. 41-46
Wife of Isaac and mother of Jacob and Esau, denied by your husband yet faithful to him, woman of discernment and independent thought. Pray with us that we may use our insights with courage, particularly when striving for peace and justice in family life.

Jacob (Israel)   Esau

Reuben   Simeon   Issachar   Zebulun

Levi   Judah

Dinah
Genesis 30:21; 34:1-26
Daughter of Jacob and victim of rape, regarded by her brothers as "defiled" and used by them as an excuse for pillage and ethnic massacre. Pray for us and for all who are in any way marginalised and abused.

Deborah
Judges 4:1-24; 5:24-31
Wise counsellor and leader of men, a mother of Israel delivering, with the woman Jael, your people from enemy oppression. Pray for us and for all who need to exercise leadership with wisdom and justice.

Tamar
Genesis 38:6-30
Childless widow, treated as a prostitute by the self-righteous Judah, then mother of twins, thus becoming the ancestor of Jesus, "son of David of the tribe of Judah". Pray for us and for all who make hasty false judgements.

Er   Onan   Shelagh

Perez   Zerah

Mary
Mother of Jesus, fruit of the experience of women in Israel, we simply greet you and your son Jesus:

Mary the dawn, and Christ the light of day!
Mary the gate, and Christ the heavenly way!
Mary the root, and Christ the mystic vine!
Mary the grape, and Christ the sacred wine!
Mary the beacon, Christ the harbour's rest!
Mary the mirror, Christ the vision blest!

Woman of love, who Son of God conceived!
Woman of faith, blest since you first believed!
Woman of sorrow, standing by the cross!
Woman of prayer, with Church at Pentecost!
Mother of Christ, our brother, friend and king!
Mother of God, with you to God we sing!

(first verse from literary executors of Canon J. Fennelly)

Hannah
1 Samuel 1:1-18; 2:1-10
Suffering for many years the curse of barrenness in a society where a woman's worth was measured by the number of her sons, scolded by the priest and judged to be intoxicated when you dared to pray in a sacred place, mother of the prophet Samuel who anointed the first kings of Israel. Pray for us and for all who are harshly judged by religious people.

Digging deeper into the past in the light of the present

It may seem strange now, at the end of our Old Testament journey, to be going back to the book of Genesis. But since we have now covered the main features of the "map" of the Hebrew Bible, it seems a pretty good place to begin to reflect on our journey in a deeper way.

The first eleven chapters of Genesis present us with fascinating parables. (Remember no one was sitting there at the time of creation, pen in hand, all poised to write down the story for us!)

You will soon be invited to refresh your memory by reading the key passages. As you do so, please take your time, making sacred space for your reflections in the presence of God, and exploring the relevance of each passage for life today.

The priest's story

But before you do this, imagine one of the Hebrew priests in exile in Babylon. By this time the Hebrews had been delivered from slavery in Egypt, and they had settled in the Promised Land, before eventually being evicted into exile in Babylon.

Imagine this exiled Hebrew priest looking out from his little house, gazing thoughtfully at the very sophisticated society all around him, a city that was buzzing with activity, full of the signs of success and wealth, its inhabitants seemingly imbued with a self-esteem and drive that did not need the Hebrew God. Morality everywhere around was based on power: "I have, therefore I am."

The priest was challenged by disturbing questions: Are we poor exiles really the chosen people? Does God still have a special love for us? Has our God been beaten at last? Is our God still in charge? Anyway, who needs God in these modern times?

The priest hears about a Babylonian creation myth:

"Once upon a time, there were two gods, a male god, Marduk, and a female god, Tiamat. They had a quarrel, so the male god inflated Tiamat so that she became a great balloon. He threw her into the sky and hurled his spear at her. She exploded in a Big Bang… and the pieces began to settle. On the first day, this and that appeared. On the second day something else…"

The priest thought: "They've got it all wrong! In the beginning there were not two gods – there was only God! Yes, our Hebrew God was in charge! On the first day there was light. And it was our God who separated the light from the darkness. On the second day God, our God, separated the waters above from the waters below. And so on…"

We can see how the priest took an existing mythical picture of creation and "baptised" it to tell the Hebrews that their God was the Creator. God was there in the beginning and God had been in charge all the time. But why were they all now in exile? Well, that was because of human pride, bitterness, superstition and self-will.

Once human pride had asserted itself then vengeance, like that of Cain and Lamech, began to spread like a disease and dis-ease was felt. (Lamech was a descendant of Cain, and in 4:23-24 the writer tells us that if Cain had taken sevenfold vengeance, then Lamech's searching for vengeance, several generations later, would be much worse.) The people began to be self-important and superstitious, and presume too much upon God's protection even when they were doing evil things to their daughters, so God sent a flood to remind them of God's desire to save them. Then they began to feel so self-sufficient that they thought they did not need God and they took great pride in their huge building projects. So God brought about babbling confusion to teach them a lesson, if they would but listen: "Therefore it was called Babel, because there the Lord confused the language of all the earth" (11:9).

The priest looked around him and said, "Where are you, God?" And he began to find the answers as he reflected on his experience as a Hebrew.

The priest thought about how God had reached out to God's people through Abraham and the patriarchs like Isaac and Jacob and Joseph; how God had once before delivered them from slavery and exile under the powerful, sophisticated rulers of Egypt. God had done it once. But could God do it again? And what had gone wrong, to get us into this miserable state of exile?

With the priest, we too could look around us and "peel the onion of life" as we see it. (See the diagram on the next page.) Working from the outside of the Genesis parables, starting at Genesis 11:1-9, we can see the veneer of the city's Godless pride. Peeling into the next layer, 6:1-8, we see the cause of the Flood: men's self-importance and superstition, their feeling that they could do what they liked with women, since they were "sons of God". At a deeper level still, 4:15 and 4:23, we see how bitterness of heart only increases if we insist on vengeance. Then, moving deeper, we get back to the "Adam" in each one of us, 3:1-14, where we put ourselves on a pedestal above God and *we* decide what's what! When we have peeled all these layers away, we finally arrive at the God within: "in the beginning… GOD!" Here is the neglected core. This negligence is the root cause of the Hebrews' going astray. *That* is what went wrong!

That reflection is still valid for our twenty-first-century civilisation. Genesis 1–11 may have the literary form of parables, but the parables are surely true to life.

So now we could examine in our Bibles the texts shown in our diagram, reading them from the context we have just outlined and seeing what relevance this has for our times today.

Peeling the onion of Genesis

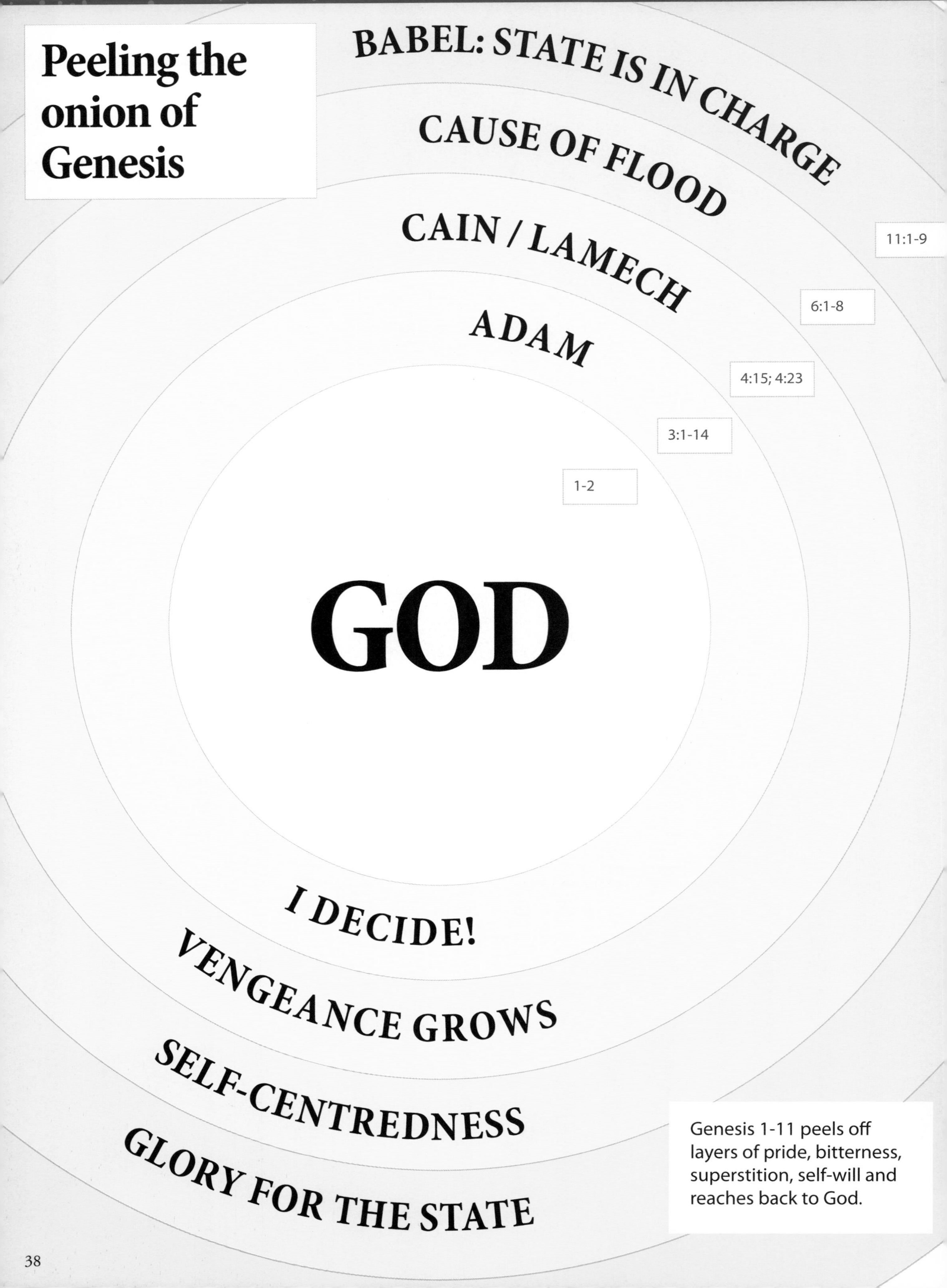

BABEL: STATE IS IN CHARGE

CAUSE OF FLOOD

CAIN / LAMECH

ADAM

GOD

11:1-9

6:1-8

4:15; 4:23

3:1-14

1-2

I DECIDE!

VENGEANCE GROWS

SELF-CENTREDNESS

GLORY FOR THE STATE

Genesis 1-11 peels off layers of pride, bitterness, superstition, self-will and reaches back to God.

The "J" source of Genesis

You will perhaps remember that the priestly tradition in the Law was only one of its four main sources. We referred on pages 10-11 to these traditions as J, P, D and E. Well, the last two – D and E – have not had any significant influence on the Genesis parables that we have been studying in this section. But J does have its own special (and very early) way of describing the creation story and the fall of humankind in Genesis 2 and 3. J writes in Jerusalem, long before the priests in exile in Babylon, though J's story of the creation comes second in the Bible, after P's great hymn in Genesis 1:1 – 2:2. The priests seem to have decided this as sacred writings began to be put together after the exile.

The civil servant's story

Let us reflect a little on this J story and imagine its writer now. He might well tell his circumstances like this:

"I am a civil servant in the court of King David. I am one of a group of people who were instructed by the king to prepare the official state version of our traditions. Now that we were a kingdom and had civil servants like me who were able to write, the king felt that we should be like other respectable nations and have our traditions put into writing. Previously we had just handed them down by word of mouth.

"My job was specially to put into writing the early traditions we had about the creation by God.

"The main story we had, which was handed down from one generation to the next, was about the creation of *human beings*. Children would ask: Where do we come from? Women would ask: Why is childbirth so painful? Others would ask: Why do snakes have to crawl around on the ground? Others: Why do we have to die? Others again: Why can we not do just anything we want?

"Our creation story covered many of these questions.

"In the beginning God made a beautiful garden. In it there were two trees: the tree of life, whose fruits brought immortality; and the tree of knowledge, whose fruits gave the ability to decide for ourselves what was good or what was evil. This tree was not for us. God kept this one. But the tree of life and the beautiful garden were made especially for us. God breathed God's own breath of life into the dust there and made man and woman, equal in dignity and equal in responsibility. And then we blew it!

"That is what I had to put into writing for the royal records in Jerusalem."

The journey continues

I hope our study so far has helped to highlight the main features of our Old Testament. We have touched upon key events in a long journey from God's revelation to Abraham, through the story of Moses and the covenant, and then through stories of kings and prophets into the experience of exile, followed by the return from Babylon and the rebuilding of the Temple.

We saw that four main traditions have been slotted together in the Law; then histories and prophetic writings have been passed on; the Psalms and books of Wisdom have followed and been added to this great religious library. This is the only Bible that Jesus knew. Now we are poised to continue the journey into the Gospel story of Jesus, and into his influence on others as the promised Messiah of the Old Testament that we have been studying. The journey continues!

THE

TESTAMENT

40 BC	27 BC	c. 6 BC	4 BC	c. AD 8	AD 14	c. 26	c. 30-33	c. 31-34	c. 35	c. 40-51	c. 49
Herod the Great elected King of Judea by the Roman Senate	Caesar Augustus becomes Emperor of Rome	Birth of Jesus	Death of Herod	Birth of Saul (Paul) at Tarsus	Death of Caesar Augustus; Tiberius becomes Emperor of Rome	Jesus begins public ministry	Death and resurrection of Jesus; Pentecost and beginning of the Church	St Stephen becomes first martyr	Paul's conversion on road to Damascus	Paul's mission to Cyprus and Asia Minor	The Council of Jerusalem on n[…] for circumcision

The time of JESUS   *The oral tradition (over thirty years)*

THE NEW TESTAMENT STORY

As with the earlier Hebrew story, so too the Christian story developed through events, oral tradition and writing. There was "the Jesus of history", the real human Jesus who healed, taught, died and was raised. This was followed by years of oral tradition, before Paul's letters, and then the four Gospels, were written. In the New Testament, we see how the gradual revelation of God's love in the Old Testament came to be fulfilled in the life, death and resurrection of Jesus.

The dating of the Christian era as "AD" was introduced about the year 527 by Dionysius Exiguus, a Roman monk. According to his calculations, Jesus was born 753 years after the founding of the city of Rome, and so the years numbered "AD" start at that date. Many scholars think that the calculation of Dionysius was incorrect, and that the birth of Christ really occurred a few years earlier than he placed it.

The New Testament opens with four "Gospels". Each of these tells, in different ways, the story of Jesus, and presents it as Good News (which is what the word "Gospel" means) for the communities the Gospel is written for. The Gospels detail the circumstances of Jesus' birth, his baptism in the River Jordan by John the Baptist, Jesus' calling of the apostles and his public ministry. They tell of the years he spent travelling around teaching about God, healing those who were sick and performing miracles such as turning water into wine at the wedding in Cana. Jesus' teaching led him into conflict with the religious authorities of his day, and so the Gospels also tell of his arrest and trial, and ultimately his death on the cross. They tell us of his resurrection from the dead after three days, and of his ascension into heaven.

After Jesus' ascension, the disciples gathered in the upper room, where the Spirit Jesus had promised descended upon them in tongues of fire and like a rushing wind. This happened during the Jewish feast of Pentecost, and the story is told in the book of the Acts of the Apostles. Following this event, Peter became a great charismatic preacher and thousands were baptised in Jesus' name. The established religious authorities oppressed the early Christians, but the Christians continued to tell people about Jesus and to support each other in their communities.

Although Christianity started life as a Jewish sect, the message of Jesus spread to the Gentile (non-Jewish) world rather rapidly, and one of its most famous converts was Paul, who had been an ardent persecutor of Christians. But after encountering the risen Christ on the road to Damascus in a flash of light, Paul became a prolific disciple, travelling all over the known world telling people about Jesus and writing letters of encouragement to various church communities.

Peter and Paul were in Rome during the time that the Emperor Nero was persecuting Christians, and they were both martyred there around AD 67.

The New Testament also contains letters written by other disciples, which were similarly intended to encourage and correct early Christian communities. There is the letter to the Hebrews, and the letters written by Peter, James and John, for instance. Through these letters, the communities are encouraged to remain faithful to Jesus, often in spite of very great suffering, and to avoid false teachers.

In the final book of the Bible, the Apocalypse, we see prophetic writing about the events leading up to Jesus' return. The book affirms that God is in control, that goodness will ultimately win in the struggle against darkness, and that all those whose names are written in the book of life will live for eternity in the presence of God.

c. 55	c. 58	64	c. 67	c. 65-75	c. 66-73	70	c. 80-85	c. 80-90	c. 90-100	122
New Testament ment written: first letter to alonians	Peter goes to church communities in Rome	Paul arrested in Caesarea and deported to Rome	Great Fire of Rome	Peter and Paul executed by Emperor Nero	Gospel of Mark written	Jewish uprising	Titus captures Jerusalem and destroys Temple	Luke writes his Gospel and Acts	Gospel of Matthew written	John's Gospel completed	Building of Hadrian's Wall begins

The period of writing the Gospels

But when were things written down?

Although the New Testament begins with the four Gospels, they were actually written thirty to seventy years after the resurrection.

Peter's letters were written between AD 60 and 80. They may have been written in his name after his death by Silvanus.

Paul's letters were written to the Thessalonians (c. AD 50–52), Galatians (c. AD 54–58), Philippians (c. AD 56–57), Corinthians (c. AD 52–57), Romans (c. AD 57–58), Colossians (c. AD 61–63) and Ephesians (c. AD 61–64). He wrote two letters to Timothy (the Bishop of Ephesus) and one each to Titus and Philemon.

Mark's Gospel was written around AD 65–75 for a Christian community facing persecution by the Emperor Nero in Rome. It is for this reason that almost half of the Gospel is about the trial, passion and death of Jesus. Luke's and Matthew's Gospels were both written around AD 80–90, while John's was written a little later, c. AD 90–100, probably by John's disciples.

The book of Revelation, also known as the book of the Apocalypse, was probably written over a period of years by someone who identifies himself as "John". It is likely that a number of authors contributed to the final compilation, which emerged around AD 96–98 in Asia Minor.

Matthew (Matt or Mt)
Mark (Mk)
Luke (Lk)
John (Jn)
Acts (Ac)
Romans (Rom or Rm)
1 Corinthians (1 Cor or 1 Co)
2 Corinthians (2 Cor or 2 Co)
Galatians (Gal or Ga)
Ephesians (Eph or Ep)
Philippians (Phil or Ph)
Colossians (Col)
1 Thessalonians (1 Thess or 1 Th)
2 Thessalonians (2 Thess or 2 Th)
1 Timothy (1 Tim or 1 Tm)
2 Timothy (2 Tim or 2 Tm)
Titus (Tit or Tt)
Philemon (Phlm or Phm)
Hebrews (Heb)
James (Jas or Jm)
1 Peter (1 Pet or 1 P)
2 Peter (2 Pet or 2 P)
1 John (1 Jn)
2 John (2 Jn)
3 John (3 Jn)
Jude (Jude)
Apocalypse or Revelation (Apoc; Rev or Rv)

There are 27 books in the New Testament

While the first witnesses to Jesus' life, ministry, death and resurrection were dying off, either through martyrdom or old age, it became important to have the preached story of Jesus written down. This is how our four Gospels arose.

We read in St Luke:

"Since many have undertaken to set down an orderly account of the events that have been fulfilled among us, just as they were handed on to us by those who from the beginning were eyewitnesses and servants of the word, I too decided, after investigating everything carefully from the very first, to write an orderly account for you…" (1:1-3)

The four Gospels are rooted in what the disciples saw and heard in Jesus' company and in his appearances to them after his resurrection. Along with other early writings, like the letters of Paul, they became the "AD" bit of our Bible. They are known as the canonical scriptures: the Gospels and letters that are part of the Church's official collection of sacred books.

There are four Gospels, and only four – Matthew, Mark, Luke and John. These canonical Gospels were written during the "apostolic" period, while the apostles or their immediate disciples were still living. This can be deduced from references to them by Christian writers of the following generation. They used excerpts taken only from these four canonically recognised Gospels.

The first Gospel seems to have been that of Mark, or perhaps a Hebrew or Aramaic version of Matthew – somewhat shorter than the one we actually have. The other three imitated Mark's general style. But, in doing this, each evangelist chose some things from among the many that were handed on, and tailored it all for the benefit of his immediate hearers.

These four Gospels were regarded as "apostolic". They were received and handed on as from the apostles or their immediate disciples – Mark being a disciple of Peter, and Luke of Paul.

By the end of the second century, writings emerged which we know as the "apocryphal gospels". There are about fifty of them. These continued to be written throughout the first two to three hundred years after Jesus. They are full of stories of a legendary or fantastical nature. "Apocryphal" originally meant "secret", or "hidden". Some of these apocryphal gospels seem to have had their origins in an elitist group of Christians who thought they had special insights from God about Jesus. They wrote these down and circulated them among themselves as their own secret knowledge. Other apocryphal gospels were probably pious inventions, built around an element of tradition to help devotion, rather like some of our "nativity" plays or the mystery plays in the Middle Ages. The Church never accepted them as part of the genuine apostolic tradition, even though they claimed to have been written by one of the disciples or other contemporaries like Pilate.

Around AD 170 a scholarly monk called Tatian decided that it was far too confusing for us to have four Gospels. So he harmonised them in a way that appealed to him personally and produced his own "Gospel". It was called the Diatessaron (literally "through four into one"). It was used in the Syrian Church for some four hundred years. Elsewhere the Church stressed the value of having our four distinct ways of appreciating God's love in Jesus. St Irenaeus of Lyons, some twenty years after Tatian's publication, expressly insisted on the use of all four Gospels, since each gave its own insights or portrait of Jesus. His influence was notable, and it is significant that he is recognised as a saint by both the Eastern Orthodox Church and the Church in Rome. In due course, especially after 423, the Diatessaron fell out of use in Syria when a bishop there, Theodoret, declared Tatian to have been a heretic, banned the use of his work and ordered the destruction of the two hundred copies he was able to lay his hands on!

Each Gospel gives us a valuable but different portrait of Jesus. Imagine the exhibition of a valuable diamond in the middle of a room. When we look at it from one aspect, then we see one special insight. As we move to another part of the room, we can appreciate a different valuable feature. The four Gospels give us four portraits of Jesus, but we can see each of the Gospels as the result of a three-stage process:

- Jesus in his human lifetime;
- Jesus as preached in the various early communities with their differing needs;
- and Jesus as described *in the writings* about him a generation or more later.

WHY DO WE SAY BC AND AD?

The question has been asked: Why do we say BC (Before Christ) and then AD (Anno Domini)? Why don't we follow the BC bit with a similar AC (After Christ)?

One simple response could be that before Jesus was born there was the time of Jewish expectation for a Messiah (or, in Greek, a Christ). But at the end of the life of Jesus on earth something happened that changed things enormously: an event took place that transformed his followers so that they went out and preached him as the risen Lord.

Not only did they teach about him but also, when they could have run away, they were prepared to be martyred for him. In due course, from the date of the birth of Christ, any year became known as "Anno Domini", "in the year of the Lord": that is, each year was now a year in the presence of the risen Lord!

Very early in the life of the new community, the eyewitnesses to the risen Lord began to reflect on the "BC" bit of scripture – the Old Testament. They started to see how the gradual revelation of God's love in these writings came to be fulfilled in the life, death and resurrection of the Lord.

"Change your mind!" says Jesus at the start of Mark's Gospel. "Change your mind and believe the Good News!" The Gospel text in our Bibles usually says something like "repent and believe in the good news" (Mark 1:14), but the word "repent" is a translation of a Greek word that can, perhaps with more impact, mean "change one's mind". The surprising thing to us may be that Jesus was asking "religious" people to change their minds! He seems to have got on well with "sinners"; but when anyone asks religious people to change their way of thinking about God, then surely that person is heading for trouble!

The first Gospel

Mark's Gospel, our first Gospel, was probably written in Rome around AD 65–75.

Peter, the apostle, who of course knew Jesus, had converted Mark – whom Peter calls "my son" (1 Peter 5:13). Then Peter was killed in the persecution under the Emperor **Nero**.

The Roman historian Tacitus tells us about this persecution. It all started in the hot summer of July 64. Anyone who was important had left the city and gone to their country homes in the cooler hill country. Nero decided to clear away a slum area so that he could carry on with his building projects. A fire got out of hand and burned down a large section of the city. This is what Tacitus writes:

"Nero fastened the guilt and inflicted the most exquisite tortures on a class of people, called Christians by the populace.

"Christus, from whom the name had its origin, suffered the extreme penalty during the reign of Tiberius at the hands of one of our procurators, Pontius Pilate, and a most mischievous superstition, thus checked for the moment, again broke out, not only in Judea, the first source of the evil, but also in Rome, where all things hideous and shameful from every part of the world find their centre and become popular.

"Accordingly, an arrest was first made of all who pleaded guilty; then upon their information, an immense multitude was convicted, not so much of the crime of firing the city, as of hatred against mankind. Mockery of every sort was added to their deaths. Covered with the skins of beasts, they were torn by dogs and perished, or were nailed to crosses, or were doomed to the flames and burnt, to serve as nightly illumination when daylight had expired. Nero offered his gardens for the spectacle, and was exhibiting a show in the circus, while he mingled with the people in the dress of a charioteer or stood aloft on a vehicle."

Nero: *Roman Emperor, ruled from AD 54 to 68. A tyrant who "fiddled while Rome burned". Persecuted early Christians.*

The Gospel of Mark was written for a community cracking under persecution, with many people giving up their faith through a perfectly understandable human fear. No one wanted to be tortured and killed by Nero! It was much easier to "curse" Jesus and be set free.

Peter had cursed Jesus at one time (Mark 14:71), but with God's help he had found strength again and had given his life in martyrdom for his Lord. This offered a model for the people of Rome, a model that was based on Jesus' own example of unwavering faith in the face of death.

What Mark did was to select material from the oral tradition he had received from Peter, and arrange it to give a portrait of Jesus that these people in Rome desperately needed. It showed a picture of Jesus being gradually abandoned by the crowds, by the disciples and even by the special three (Peter, James and John), till eventually on the cross Jesus prays: "My God, my God, why have you forsaken me?" (15:34).

What Mark was saying was: if you want to be a follower of Jesus, then don't be looking for a wise philosopher or a great miracle man. The Messiah can only be properly understood from the point of view of the cross. Focus on Jesus, the crucified, seemingly abandoned by everyone, yet totally poured out in unconditional love while surrounded by darkness.

A powerful portrait

Mark's portrait of Jesus is a powerful one for anyone who is experiencing darkness and struggle in relationships. This Gospel shows us a Jesus who is misunderstood and rejected, time after time, even by those closest to him. It is only after the darkness of the crucifixion, says this writer, that we can see what Jesus is really like: someone who doggedly stood up for his convictions in the face of all possible opposition. (This is exactly what Mark's readers needed to imitate as they faced Nero's persecution in Rome.)

In fact the writer gives over almost the whole of the second half of his Gospel to the events that culminate with the trial, passion and death of Jesus. The big question for Mark's community, and for us today, is "Who do you say that I am?" (8:29). And until we see Jesus as the crucified one, who has gone through utter loneliness and darkness, we all get it wrong.

Not many of us will have settled down and read right through Mark from beginning to end in one sitting. But if we do, then we begin to see how the writer has selected his material from the eyewitnesses and preachers who told him about Jesus.

We will look at Mark's story in two ways. One way is to see the story in five stages. At the end of each stage Jesus is rejected and misunderstood – until we get to the death of Jesus. The cross shows us what God in Jesus is really like.

1. Jesus appears, preaching God's kingdom
    A. John the Baptist appears; the Jesus story begins (1:1-8)
    B. Jesus is introduced. "Change your minds!" (1:9-15)
    C. Jesus' ministry begins; he chooses disciples (1:16-20)
    D. Jesus teaches and heals (1:21-45)
    E. Jesus is rejected; he experiences conflict with religious authorities (2:1 – 3:6)

2. Jesus ministers in Galilee
    A. Jesus chooses the twelve (3:7-19)
    B. Jesus contrasts true followers with his own family (3:20-35)
    C. Jesus teaches in seed parables (4:1-34)
    D. Jesus performs mighty acts (4:35 – 5:43)
    E. Jesus is rejected; he is in conflict with his own relatives (6:1-6)

3. Jesus and the disciples move outwards in teaching and healing
    A. Jesus sends out the twelve; John is killed (6:7-29)
    B. Jesus feeds and heals (6:30-56)
    C. Jesus teaches about the Law (7:1-23)
    D. Jesus heals and feeds (7:24 – 8:10)
    E. Jesus is misunderstood by disciples and Pharisees (8:11-21)

4. Jesus is faced with blindness; he tries to teach on discipleship
    A. Jesus opens blind eyes (8:22-26)
    B. First passion prediction and reactions to this (8:27 – 9:29)
    C. Second passion prediction and the need for all to bear a cross (9:30 – 10:31)
    D. Third passion prediction and reactions to this (10:32-45)
    E. Jesus opens blind eyes to "frame" and emphasise this section 4 (10:46-52)

5. Jesus in Jerusalem
    A. Jesus appears in the Temple (11:1 – 12:44)
    B. Jesus tells of the coming end (13:1-37)
    C. Jesus' final deeds – failure of disciples to understand and support him (14:1-42)
    D. Jesus the king – failure of the authorities, who accuse him of blasphemy (14:43 – 15:38)
    E. Jesus, Son of God – successful understanding of Jesus by centurion (15:39)

Another way is to look at the following diagram of the Gospel. It shows in the first half how Jesus worked so many wonder-filled deeds. And then Jesus asks: "Who do you say I am?" Peter says that Jesus is the Messiah, all the time probably thinking of a wonder-worker who would bring in God's kingdom right away. When Peter objects to Jesus being a *suffering* Messiah, Jesus calls him "Satan". Thereafter, the crowds leave Jesus, his disciples abandon him, the special three (Peter, James and John) leave him, until finally on the cross Jesus cries out in the darkness: "My God, my God, why have you forsaken me?" Only after Jesus' going through this utter darkness and isolation does God intervene and give the signs – the tearing of the Temple curtain and the confessing of the Roman centurion: "Truly this man was God's Son!"

This was the portrait of Jesus that Mark's community needed to appreciate: trust God in the darkness of rejection and persecution. And it is "crucial" for all of us who experience the cross of rejection and isolation, or who face death and darkness today.

Mark's Gospel
The Gospel for all: to the ends of the earth!

Who do you say I am?

Blind man

Feeding 4,000

Deaf and dumb

Syrophoenician girl

Raising Jairus' daughter

Haemorrhaging woman

Gerasene demoniac

Storm calmed

Withered hand

Paralysed boy

Leper

Casts out demons

Peter's mother-in-law

Crowds leave Jesus

Disciples leave Jesus

Special three
leave Jesus

MY GOD, WHY?

From Baptism

To Death

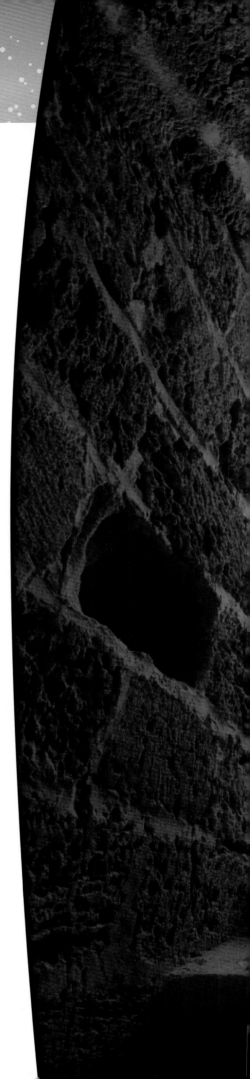

The resurrection of Christ is at the centre of our faith

The four Gospels tell us what happened after the death of Jesus in different ways.

In Mark 16:1-8, the resurrection account is stark. Women come to the tomb to embalm the body; the tomb is empty; they are told by an angel to tell Peter that Jesus has gone ahead to Galilee; the women run away, afraid and saying nothing.

There is no appearance of Jesus. Just an empty tomb, and a message. This is indeed a strange way to end a Gospel, with women running away, afraid to say anything!

So let us reflect on the scene more closely.

The sabbath is over as darkness falls around 6 p.m. on that Saturday. The shops open up again for the evening. The faithful women followers from Galilee go out to buy sweet-smelling spices. They feel that, even a few days after death in that hot climate, there is still need to attend to the body (to hide the odour of decay). They obviously are not expecting a resurrection!

They find an opened, empty tomb. The body is not there. An angel gives them an astonishing message, which they are told to pass on to those poor deserters, Peter and his companions.

We might have expected the women to rush back with the joyful news. But Mark does not say this. Instead they flee full of fear, saying nothing to anyone. *And that is the end of his Gospel!*

Mark's original ending?

Although our Bibles carry a longer ending after Mark 16:8, with various appearances of the risen Christ, most scholars would agree that these were added in the second century and that the original Gospel ended as we have outlined.

The early manuscripts of the Gospel, as well as the Church Fathers – scholars who wrote in the early centuries of the Church's life, like Clement, Origen, Eusebius and Jerome – do not refer to the longer ending when we might expect them to do so. The manuscripts of Mark that they used seem to have stopped at verse 8 of chapter 16. Moreover, the style of language and vocabulary used from verse 9 onwards is different from the rest of Mark.

So did Mark intend to end his Gospel at verse 8, or is it unfinished for some other reason?

Mark might have died before completing it, possibly in the persecution of Christians carried out by Nero. Perhaps a longer ending, with one resurrection appearance, or several, may have been lost before it was copied. The Gospel does appear to end in mid-sentence, suggesting that there was something intended to follow it.

Many scholars argue that Mark really intended to finish at verse 8. That causes the Gospel to end on a note of fear, awe and amazement.

This was the way that Mark ended other sections – the stilling of the storm, the transfiguration and several of the miracles. The reaction indicates a bewildered lack of understanding of what God is doing in Jesus.

Such a message is just what Mark's Roman audience needed; not lots of easy signs and miracles to get them through the darkness of persecution. Their great leaders Peter and Paul were dead.

In the ensuing dark days the message was to go forward in faith – "Go… and you will see him!" No point in looking for miracles round every corner.

Here was the instruction to any followers who were tempted to be disloyal in the face of fearful persecution. In spite of all, Jesus still called them to be followers, through the darkness, as he too experienced it in facing up to death.

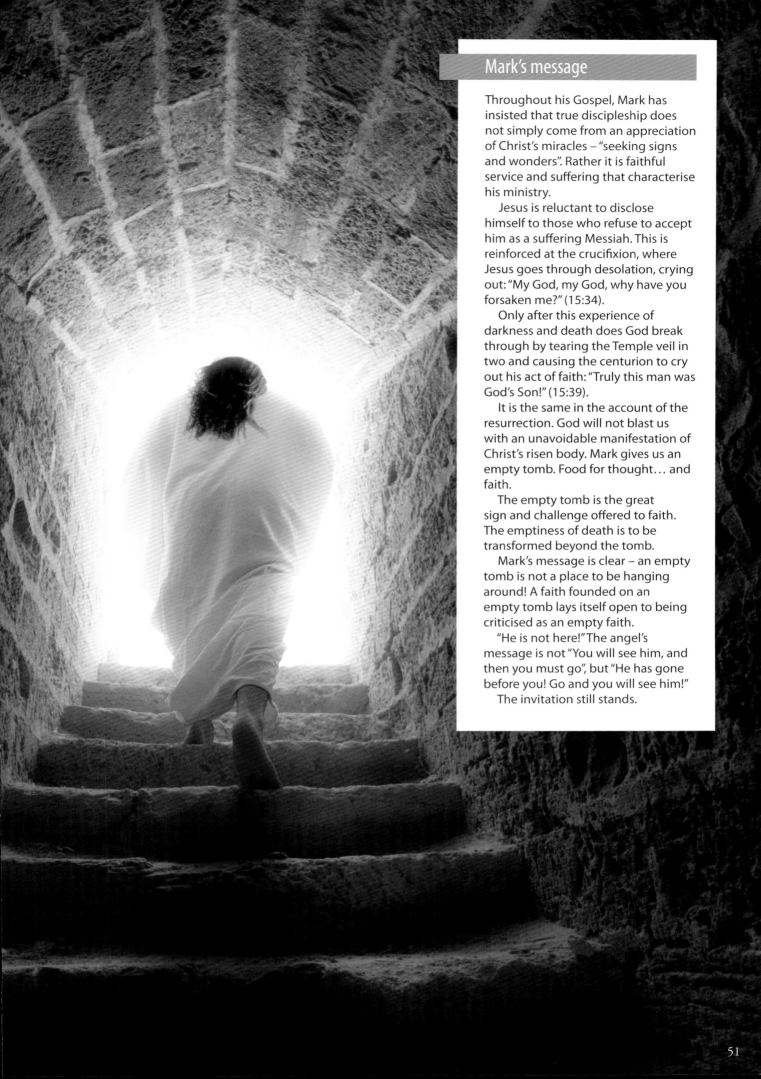

Mark's message

Throughout his Gospel, Mark has insisted that true discipleship does not simply come from an appreciation of Christ's miracles – "seeking signs and wonders". Rather it is faithful service and suffering that characterise his ministry.

Jesus is reluctant to disclose himself to those who refuse to accept him as a suffering Messiah. This is reinforced at the crucifixion, where Jesus goes through desolation, crying out: "My God, my God, why have you forsaken me?" (15:34).

Only after this experience of darkness and death does God break through by tearing the Temple veil in two and causing the centurion to cry out his act of faith: "Truly this man was God's Son!" (15:39).

It is the same in the account of the resurrection. God will not blast us with an unavoidable manifestation of Christ's risen body. Mark gives us an empty tomb. Food for thought… and faith.

The empty tomb is the great sign and challenge offered to faith. The emptiness of death is to be transformed beyond the tomb.

Mark's message is clear – an empty tomb is not a place to be hanging around! A faith founded on an empty tomb lays itself open to being criticised as an empty faith.

"He is not here!" The angel's message is not "You will see him, and then you must go", but "He has gone before you! Go and you will see him!"

The invitation still stands.

Outsiders in Jesus' family tree

We have seen how the Old Testament begins with Genesis. But it may come as a surprise to learn that the New Testament also begins with Genesis. This is what Matthew calls Jesus' family tree – "The Genesis of Jesus Christ, Son of David, Son of Abraham" (Matthew 1:1). We need to remember that Matthew wrote in Greek and that some of the nuances in his work can get lost in the English translation. Your Bible text may have "the genealogy of Jesus", but the Greek word for "genealogy" is the same one used for the word "genesis", so Matthew may well be hinting that there is a new Genesis here with the coming of Jesus – and that all this is part of God's great plan from the very beginning.

If you ever try to read Matthew's Gospel you will probably have a problem getting started. For the writer begins with the family tree of Jesus, with its great list of names, including patriarchs and strangely named kings, most of whom you may never have heard of.

But if you look closely, you may notice how the writer outlines the three big stages of Hebrew history: from Abraham to King David; from David to the exile in Babylon; and from the exile to Christ. Matthew stresses that there are fourteen generations in each of these periods.

It helps to know that you can write "fourteen" in Hebrew as "DVD", which can also sound like the Hebrew for "David". So, in a symbolic way, by writing "fourteen, fourteen, fourteen", Matthew is really also writing "David, David, David".

This is a clever literary device for telling us that Jesus – in a greater way than David, of course – is destined to be king.

Matthew's training college

It seems that Matthew's Gospel arose in a large prosperous city like Antioch in Syria. Possibly Matthew the apostle had gone there and taught about Jesus. By AD 100, **Ignatius of Antioch** tells us that the Church there used what we now call the Gospel of Matthew, although the Gospel itself doesn't say who wrote it. It was Bishop Papias in the second century who called this Gospel after Matthew and there is no serious reason to doubt that the apostle Matthew was the *authority* behind it. But the *final author*, the actual writer of this Gospel, seems to have used three sources for the work: he used most of Mark; he incorporated a collection of the sayings of Jesus; and he included a great amount of material that we find only in this Gospel, material that came in part from someone we call Matthew.

It contained so much *teaching* about Jesus that it quickly became used all over the Church as its "first" Gospel. (That is why we find it at the beginning of our New Testament, although it was written *after* Mark.) It was seen to be first in importance.

It is easy to imagine the challenges to the early Church in Antioch. Here there was a large, prosperous city containing many Jews and Gentiles, many opinions, and indeed there arose many outlandish tales about Jesus, which we can read about in the **apocryphal gospels.** The Church already had Mark's Gospel with its picture of the many *actions* of Jesus. But what it seriously needed now was clear *teaching* about Jesus.

Ignatius of Antioch: *leader of the Church in Antioch, Syria, teaching, writing and setting a firm line for the official leadership of bishops. Martyred in Rome by being thrown to the lions in the Colosseum in AD 108.*

Apocryphal gospels: *writings of early Christians about Jesus, by people associated with him like Pilate or St James. Not seen as official teaching since they are often fanciful or legendary exaggerations.*

The person who finally put this Gospel together was a brilliant teacher. This evangelist used all the usual tricks to assist the memory of his new catechists or "church teachers". He used groups of seven: the seven petitions of the Lord's Prayer (unlike Luke's version); the seven woes in chapter 23; the seven parables in chapter 13 and so on. Notice how he *selected* these sevens from the oral tradition and put them together in one place. It is not as though Jesus went out one day and taught seven parables on the trot. They have been *collected together* by the author for a purpose: to help catechists remember easily, using the Jewish perfect number, seven. A Gospel is not originally a life story: it is an *arrangement* of materials, selected from the oral tradition, and shaped to suit the pastoral needs of a particular community. Matthew's community needed sound teaching. This prosperous community was able to pay for the writing of the Gospel of Matthew. We may call "Matthew" the "Teacher's Gospel".

As well as having sevens, the evangelist also gave us threes to assist memory: the three groups in the family tree in chapter 1; the three types of piety in 6:1-18, namely prayer, almsgiving and fasting; the three "argumentative" parables in 21:28 – 22:14 ("When the chief priests and Pharisees heard his parables, they realised that he was speaking about them").

Elsewhere the writer has collections of ten: there are ten miracles beginning at chapter 8. Again, it is not as if Jesus went out one day and worked ten miracles. This is a *collection*, brought together by the writer to assist the training of catechists in his church. Among his sixty or so references to the Hebrew scriptures he has a separate twelve, the special "fulfilment" quotations from the Old Testament, which he identifies for his readers as being: "to fulfil what had been spoken by the Lord through the prophet…" (1:22; 2:17 and so on). These are Matthew's direct quotations from the Hebrew scriptures, which he explicitly claims to be fulfilled in Jesus.

To get our bearings it is often useful to have a "map" of a Gospel. Several possibilities arise, but the commonest one is to see this Gospel as having five large sections or "books" at its heart. The evangelist was a good teacher: he knew how to work from the known to the unknown. His disciples knew about Moses and the five "books of Moses" (the first five books of our Old Testament). So he taught that Jesus was in some ways like a second Moses, and he gave his catechists these five blocks of material to learn as part of their training. We can detect the seams between the blocks by noticing, at the end of each block, the phrase "When Jesus had finished saying these things" (7:28; 11:1; 13:53; 19:1; 26:1). And each block contains two things: it has an account of actions of Jesus, taken mainly from Mark, followed by a teaching sermon of Jesus. (See the diagram opposite.) You can imagine the writer saying to his catechists, "I would like you to learn thoroughly the first book about Jesus in Galilee and about his basic teaching, the Sermon on the Mount. When you know this, come back to me and we'll see if you're ready to go on to the second stage."

In book two the catechists will learn about ten miracles of Jesus and also his teaching about how to be a true apostle. The third section, the middle of the five (and perhaps the most important), is for the catechists to learn how Jesus dealt with opposition from the **Pharisees** and to know the seven parables about the kingdom of heaven. At the heart of this Gospel is teaching on the kingdom of heaven.

Matthew's Gospel is the only one to mention "church". This occurs in section four where we hear about Jesus training Peter and giving the great sermon on forgiveness:

"Then Peter came and said to him, 'Lord, if another member of the church sins against me, how often should I forgive? As many as seven times?' Jesus said to him, 'Not seven times, but, I tell you, seventy-seven times.'" (18:21-22)

The final "book" moves on to the theme of judgement and the end of time. All five "books" are sandwiched between a section on the infancy drama at the start of the Gospel and the trial, death and resurrection of Jesus at the end – making a grand total of *seven* sections.

So we begin to see that the Gospel of Matthew is not just a book on a shelf, or even a section of our church lectionary. It arose from real people needing to appreciate Jesus as the great teacher. Only in Matthew do we hear Jesus teaching about the parables of the weeds among the wheat; the unforgiving servant; the workers in the vineyard; the two sons; the ten bridesmaids; and the sheep and the goats… and so much more!

There is much teaching about Peter, especially about him trying to walk on water, and his problems about forgiveness and receiving the power of the keys. There is much concern too about Judas in this Gospel, perhaps because the name "Judas" means "the Jew" (just as the name "Scott" today gives us a link with Scotland), and this emerging Church was having problems in its relationship with Judaism. While at times in our history this Gospel has been used as an excuse for anti-Semitism, we can surely do much better than that and focus on its portrait of Jesus as the teacher par excellence, the one who said:

"Come to me, all you that are weary and are carrying heavy burdens, and I will give you rest. Take my yoke upon you, and learn from me; for I am gentle and humble in heart, and you will find rest for your souls. For my yoke is easy, and my burden is light." (11:28-30)

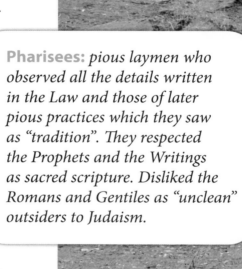

Pharisees: *pious laymen who observed all the details written in the Law and those of later pious practices which they saw as "tradition". They respected the Prophets and the Writings as sacred scripture. Disliked the Romans and Gentiles as "unclean" outsiders to Judaism.*

Matthew – The Teacher's Gospel

CONCLUSION: Trial, death and resurrection of Jesus

Narrative: Increased opposition

Judgement

Teaching: Sermon on the future
19:2 – 26:1

Five

Narrative: Jesus trains Peter

The Church

Teaching: Sermon on order / forgiveness
13:54 – 19:1

Four

Narrative: Opposition of Pharisees

The Kingdom

Teaching: Seven parables of the kingdom
11:2 – 13:53

Three

Narrative: Ten miracles of power and love

Discipleship

Teaching: The apostolic sermon
8:1 – 11:1

Two

Narrative: Jesus' Galilean ministry

The New Law

Teaching: Sermon on the Mount
3:1 – 7:29

One

INTRODUCTION: The infancy drama about Jesus

LUKE: GOOD NEWS FOR EVERYONE

Luke is a favourite Gospel for many people. Maybe this is because it contains the word "joy" or "rejoice" more than any other Gospel. (Luke uses "joy" ten times more than Mark and "rejoice" six times more than Matthew. But Mark never uses the word "rejoice", since, as you may remember, Mark is mainly concerned with Jesus' struggle through the darkness of misunderstandings and the path of the cross.) Other favourite topics for Luke include prayer, table sharing, the valuing of seemingly "unimportant" people, and the role of the Holy Spirit.

This is the only Gospel to contain some of our favourite parables: the good Samaritan (where "outsiders" are seen to be OK, as we find also in the story of the ten lepers); the unforgettable images in the three reconciliation parables of chapter 15 – the lost sheep, the woman's lost coin, and the prodigal son (which I prefer to call "the lost sons", since both of them were "lost"; not just the one who left home and returned a wiser person, but also the one who stayed at home, kept all the rules and regulations, and thought that, because of this, his father owed him something in return. Of course, God is a God of grace who owes us nothing but reaches out in love to everyone).

Another reason this Gospel attracts many of us is the way that *feelings* come through: only this Gospel tells us of Jesus' "agony" and sweating during his earnest prayer on the Mount of Olives, with the angel coming and giving him strength, just as an athlete is thoroughly warmed up before the great contest. This is the only passion account in which Jesus prays with feeling for his persecutors: "Father, forgive them; for they do not know what they are doing" (23:34). Only in this Gospel do we find someone intimately addressing Jesus simply as "Jesus", without any formal title added – "Jesus, remember me when you come into your kingdom" – and we read of Jesus' unconditional reply: "Today you will be with me in Paradise" (23:42-43). ("Today" is a favourite word in Luke.)

And we cannot fail to notice the feelings of the two disciples on the road to Emmaus after the death of Jesus: their "burning hearts" after meeting the risen Lord, their amazement when they recognise him in the breaking of bread, their excitement and growing confidence as they return to Peter and the women in Jerusalem.

Many of us enjoy especially the two chapters at the very beginning of Luke's Gospel, with the two **annunciations** (one to Zechariah and another to Mary), the visitation to Elizabeth, the journey from Nazareth for the birth of Jesus, the story of the shepherds and the song of the angels… and so on. Only in Luke do we find these particular "portraits" of Jesus, painted as they are with so many Old Testament pigments.

Who was Luke?

There is a man by the name of Luke who is referred to in three of Paul's letters:

- "Do your best to come to me soon… Only Luke is with me." (2 Timothy 4:9-11)
- "Luke, the beloved physician, and Demas greet you." (Colossians 4:14)
- "Epaphras, my fellow-prisoner in Christ Jesus, sends greetings to you, and so do Mark, Aristarchus, Demas, and Luke, my fellow-workers." (Philemon 23-24)

We can sense that Luke was a Gentile, because in Colossians 4:10-11 Paul says that the only Jews who worked with him were Aristarchus, Mark and Justus, so Luke was probably a Gentile, a non-Jew.

An ecumenical Gospel?

Luke, of course, was not one of the twelve apostles, but he says in his introduction that he received information from "those who from the beginning were eyewitnesses and servants of the word" (1:2).

Some scholars would say that Luke was a Gentile missionary who, in his travels, came across at least four communities or traditions, with their own distinctive pieties and "portraits" of Jesus. Luke seems to have been keen to show that Christ was bigger than any one of these "denominations"; Luke's Gospel knits together the different sources he came across, with their varying portraits of Jesus. He refused to "smooth over" their differences. Luke was simply faithful to each of his sources. He was a bridge-builder and could therefore be seen as the evangelist of an "ecumenical Gospel". The central focus for everyone is always on Jesus as the Saviour, reaching out beyond the traditional "religious" limits to everyone.

There are stories about Luke hearing first-hand accounts from Mary and dying in Egypt at the age of eighty-four, but these are speculation.

Annunciation: *literally "announcing". Often refers to the angel Gabriel announcing the message to Mary about how God has chosen her to be the mother of Jesus, God's Son.*

57

It can be helpful to see this Gospel in four main stages:

1. **The infancy and childhood of Jesus (1:5 – 2:52).** After the first four verses of introduction and dedication, we have two chapters built upon the first of Luke's special sources. This material has its own peculiar "piety". By "piety" is meant the style of prayers, practices (like fasting or going on pilgrimage) and perspectives on God (stern, forgiving and so on). There is a very traditional love of the Law and the Temple. The community that produced this material also used songs in their prayer life, hymns that still have a significant place in our liturgy today: the Benedictus, the Magnificat, the Gloria and the Song of Simeon (the "Nunc Dimittis"). With poetic sensitivity Luke gives us a whole section that is profoundly coloured by Old Testament references. These people knew and used their old scriptures to understand Jesus better.

2. **Jesus prepares for and begins his ministry in the north of the country, in Galilee (3:1 – 7:50).** Jesus starts off his mission at home, in Nazareth. We see him (in chapter 4) being invited to be a reader and preacher in his home synagogue. Jesus is clear that he has been sent "to bring good news to the poor". When Jesus says he has a mission even to non-Jews, they don't want to know it, and he has to flee to Capernaum. The rest of this section shows us Jesus calling the twelve and teaching his disciples in what is often called "the Sermon on the Plain", with its four Beatitudes and the short version of the Lord's Prayer. (Contrast Matthew's "Sermon on the Mount", with its eight or nine Beatitudes and its longer version of the Our Father.) You may see notes in the margins of your Bible telling you just how frequently Luke is copying from Mark as his source in this section.

3. **The third section takes the form of a long journey to Jerusalem (8:1 – 19:27).** Beginning at 8:1, Jesus sets off "through cities and villages, proclaiming and bringing the good news of the kingdom of God". It's a busy time for him! On his way he teaches parables about the seed and the lamp; he speaks of his mother and family as hearers and doers of God's word; after a stormy trip over the sea to the land of the Gerasenes, he heals the lad possessed by demons; he crosses back to heal the daughter of Jairus and the woman with haemorrhages; he briefs his disciples on their mission; he feeds the crowd; he challenges his disciples with "Who do you say I am?" and tells them that he will be a suffering Messiah, so they too must be ready to take up their crosses each day; he takes Peter, James and John up the mountain to experience the transfiguration.

Finally, after so much activity and teaching, Jesus fixes his sights firmly on Jerusalem as his ultimate destination: "he set his face to go to Jerusalem" (9:51). Does Luke picture Jesus as someone like Luke himself, a missionary on a great journey? Upon this framework we find Luke placing many of our favourite passages, with their own joyous and reconciling "piety". It is full of stories that stress, in a relaxed and sometimes humorous way, God's love and unconditional forgiveness, and God's championing of the underdog or outsider: the good Samaritan; the ten lepers; Martha and Mary; the friend at midnight; the woman healed on the sabbath; the rich man and Lazarus; the widow and the judge; the Pharisee and the tax collector; Zacchaeus up the tree… and so on. The journey section contains lots of material like this that is found only in Luke.

Notice how Luke, and only Luke, has already told us how Jesus took women with him on his travels, and how these continued to support him from their means (8:3). It has been argued that it was these very women who preserved much of the above material after the ascension and passed their memories and feminine insights eventually on to Luke.

Scholars agree that our evangelist certainly has a high regard for the witness of women in his Gospel. Later on, Luke will particularly mention the presence of these same Galilean women near the cross (23:49) and again at the empty tomb (24:10), when they themselves become evangelists, bringers of the Good News, to the eleven apostles and the others.

4. The final section focuses us again on Jerusalem (19:28 – 24:53). We find Jesus meeting with increased hostility as he teaches in the Temple there. Jesus' own disciples just slip away from him (Luke never blames them), and when Peter denies his master, Luke characteristically notes with feeling, "the Lord turned and looked at Peter" (22:61). The reconciliation of Herod Antipas with Pilate (23:12) is mentioned only in Luke and can probably be linked with the women's testimony (see 8:3, where Joanna, who went round supporting Jesus on his mission, is called "the wife of Herod's steward Chuza"). Luke is also the only evangelist to describe the way to Calvary (again the women are important, 23:27-31). After praying for the forgiveness of his persecutors and welcoming the criminal we call the good thief, Jesus dies uttering the words of the night prayer of a faithful Jew, "Father, into your hands I commend my spirit." Jesus dies the noble death of an innocent martyr, with the centurion exclaiming, "Certainly this man was innocent" (23:46-47).

Still in Jerusalem, we see the burial of Jesus taking place; then the women and Peter find the empty tomb; and after the appearance of Jesus on the road to Emmaus, Luke mentions the appearance of the risen Lord to the disciples in Jerusalem when Jesus eats the broiled fish (24:42). As Jesus ascends into heaven they are told to remain in the city until they are "clothed with power from on high" (24:49). They will then be witnesses to preach forgiveness of sins to all the nations of the earth, beginning from Jerusalem and going to the very ends of the earth. The scene is set for Luke's second volume, the Acts of the Apostles.

When trying to pray with this Gospel, any part, of course, is valuable. But perhaps a good place to start could be with some of the verses describing Jesus' "manifesto" in Nazareth, Luke 4:16-30. Where is today's "good news to the poor!"? How do you fit in?

Luke–Acts
The Gospel for all: to the ends of the earth!

Resurrection

Jerusalem

The Journey of Jesus

Galilee

Infancy Drama

In Luke's portrait of Jesus, two well-known features appear – Jesus as table-companion and as someone on a journey.

The word "companion" means "sharing bread", from the Latin *com* (with) and *panis* (bread). As a companion, Jesus breaks bread with many people in Luke's Gospel – with Levi (5:29), Zacchaeus (19:5), the Pharisees (7:36; 11:37; 14:1) and the five thousand (9:12-17). Luke also builds his portrait of Jesus around a long journey to Jerusalem that covers ten whole chapters.

It should not come as a surprise, then, that Luke includes these features in the passion and resurrection accounts. There is the Last Supper meal, with his own special insights; and, only in Luke, the way of the cross. In the resurrection stories Luke gives us the famous journey to and from Emmaus, and the meals there and in Jerusalem.

The account of the Last Supper shows Jesus' eagerness to share this special meal with his disciples: "I have eagerly desired to eat this Passover with you before I suffer" (22:15). Here is a solemn use of the traditional covenant meal to introduce a new covenant meal and sacrifice.

Sadly, the disciples squabble about who will be the greatest, bringing an uncomfortable disunity even into this first Eucharist. Jesus tells Peter that Satan has tried to sift the disciples like wheat. In our supermarkets the flour is already finely sifted. But when it is roughly milled, as in Jesus' time, there could remain pieces of unpalatable husk or grit. Jesus paints a picture of Satan "sifting" the disciples (and we can apply it to ourselves) – seeking out the grainy weaknesses, the tendencies and addictions that he can work upon to lead us astray.

Luke depicts for us the scene in Gethsemane: Jesus prays; he sees a cup of bitterness that he must drink; the betrayal by Judas; his utter distress at the falling away of his disciples; his awareness of his awful exposure to Satan's power. Can it be the Father's will that all of this should happen? As a man, Jesus shrinks from the prospect: in this severest of temptations to run away, he prays that God's will may be done. An angel is sent to strengthen him. He prays even more intensely and his sweat falls to the ground like drops of blood.

Jesus is in agony. *Agon* originally meant the place of an athletic contest, and then the contest itself. *Agonia* is the sweat of an athlete ready for the contest. Biblical scholars have compared the strengthening angel to a trainer who warms up the competitor. Unlike the disciples who sleep – "because of grief", says Luke – Jesus is now poised like an athlete at the starting line. *Agonia* is an intense sense of purpose, a physical and psychological awareness, and a resolute approach to drinking the cup of martyrdom.

Luke's sensitivity cannot bring him to allow Judas to kiss Jesus, so we have only an attempted kiss of betrayal (22:47) and then the arrest: "… this is your hour, and the power of darkness!" (22:53).

Returning to our theme of journey, only Luke describes the way of the cross (23:26-30). It was normal custom for a condemned man to carry his own crossbeam. It must therefore be assumed that Jesus was on the point of collapsing, so the soldiers forced Simon of Cyrene to help him. Here was a black man from Africa, who had probably scraped and saved for one special Passover meal in Jerusalem. The flat blade of a Roman centurion landed on his shoulder and he found himself ordered to assist a criminal on the way to execution. Luke notes that he "followed" Jesus with a great crowd of sympathisers.

On the way of the cross, Jesus finds space to address the women of Jerusalem, to warn them of the harsh days of Roman cruelty ahead and to bless them. The presence of mourning women was recognised as an act of love. These are not the Galilean women but local women, who provided opiates for condemned men. Jesus addresses them in the form of a blessing and a warning.

The Place of the Skull

The Roman playwright Seneca, writing around the time of Jesus, says: "I have seen crosses there, not just of one kind but fashioned in many different ways: some have their victims with head down towards the ground; some impale their private parts; others stretch out their arms on the crossbeam." The historian **Josephus** reports that Roman soldiers under Titus nailed their prisoners in different postures. Occasionally just an upright stake was used with the hand being nailed above the head. There was also a "crooked" or X-shaped cross.

With the help of Simon of Cyrene, Jesus carried a crossbeam. This could be fixed to the vertical post in two ways: a V-shaped notch was sometimes cut into the very top of the upright post and the crossbeam laid across it, giving an overall T-shape. Another type of cross had the notch cut into the side of the vertical pole at some distance from the top, and the crossbeam inserted into this. Often the cross was low enough for animals to savage the feet of the crucified. Three of the Gospels tell of the (short) rod of hyssop being used to reach the mouth of Jesus. So a reasonable guess is that the cross was about seven feet high.

Luke is not concerned with any of this. He stresses two things – the prayers and the political innocence of Jesus.

Jesus prays for the forgiveness of his tormentors. And his final prayer is the night prayer of the pious Jew, Psalm 31, which his mother probably taught him as a child going to sleep.

But here Jesus adds the word "Abba" – "Father, into your hands I commend my spirit."

Between these two prayers the repentant criminal does something never heard of in the Gospels – he addresses Jesus by his first name: "Jesus, remember me when you come into your kingdom." In the eyes of the world, both have sunk as low as you could expect. Familiarity breaks through the boundaries of respectability and status. Jesus welcomes the "deathbed" conversion: "Today you will be with me in Paradise." Luke never calls the criminal "good" or a "thief"; the only thing the man seems to "steal" is Paradise.

After the death, Luke reminds us of the innocence of Jesus. The centurion exclaims: "Certainly this man was innocent", thus affirming the political blamelessness of Jesus as stated three times by Pilate, once by Herod and once again by the repentant criminal. This is important for Luke's Roman reader, Theophilus (1:3), and for all political leaders in the Roman missionary territory of around AD 80.

See the effect of the death that Luke gives us: the criminal repents; the centurion praises God; the crowds leave grieving, perhaps preparing their hearts for the later preaching which converted so many (Acts 2:41). Then there are the faithful followers who stand at a distance. These are male acquaintances, as Luke and only Luke says (though this is not apparent in many English translations of the Greek masculine word that Luke uses). Was Peter among them, following the "look" of Jesus towards him after he had denied his master three times (22:61)? Luke then specially mentions the women from Galilee, also at a distance. (Perhaps they were not permitted to approach any nearer, since there was a ban in AD 31 on even relatives approaching the process of execution.)

Josephus: *a Jewish historian of the first century. He wrote about the Jewish rebellion against Rome and the destruction of Jerusalem in AD 70.*

Nourishment anew

Luke gives us three resurrection stories: the women's journey to the tomb, the Emmaus journey and meal, and the communal "fish supper" in Jerusalem on the way to the final commissioning and ascension – only Luke mentions the ascension.

Our prayer today may be that Jesus may open our eyes to the nail scars in his risen body around us and within us. May he take us and bless us to be ourselves a journeying church where our bread is broken daily for others. In this way, may we become more active participants in his living body in our neighbourhood, as with his inspiration and guidance we work to build up his kingdom of love, peace and justice today.

The journey goes on. To be effective pilgrim people we are always in need of nourishment.

LUKE: RESURRECTION AND ASCENSION

It may come as a surprise to learn that the ascension (and Pentecost) are only mentioned by one Gospel writer: Luke. You will not find these in Mark or Matthew or John. Writing around AD 80–85, only Luke gives us in dramatic form the stories of Pentecost and the ascension.

It comes as a further surprise to some readers that Luke has two differing ways of presenting the ascension. In his Gospel, Luke tells us that the risen Lord "was carried up into heaven" on Easter Sunday evening. But in his other work, the Acts of the Apostles, Jesus ascends into heaven forty days *after* Easter.

Scholars have different explanations for this apparent disparity. Some would say that Luke is recording two of the different accounts he found in the early preaching about the ascension. He put one at the end of his Gospel and the other in his second volume, the Acts of the Apostles.

Others, perhaps more plausibly, would argue that as he got towards the end of the writing of his Gospel, Luke simply ran out of room! That is not as mad as it may seem. To write a lengthy work, like a Gospel, you needed to go to the shop and buy a scroll of papyrus or parchment. The normal length of such a scroll would be about twenty-two feet. So, it could be argued, Luke had written so much about the infancy and the great journey of Jesus that he needed to complete his Gospel quickly by seeing the resurrection completed with the ascension.

But when it came to writing his second volume, the account of the Spirit in the early Church, Luke had a brand new scroll to work with, and so he had the space to tell us about the forty days in which the risen Lord supported the work of the early community. Both accounts are true: at the resurrection, Jesus of course "was carried up into heaven" (Luke 24:51); and after forty days of supporting the early community, Jesus "was lifted up, and a cloud took him out of their sight" (Acts 1:9).

Reading with biblical eyes

Some of us are old enough to remember how the first Russian cosmonaut, speeding above the clouds, claimed that there was no sight of God up there. That prompts us to ask: Did Jesus really go *upwards through the clouds?* We need to read Luke's text with biblical eyes. Throughout scripture, the cloud is the symbol of God's presence (for example, Exodus 24:15-18; but see also Luke 9:34 at the transfiguration). It's not possible to describe God in visual terms, so one way was to use this symbol of the cloud. This helps us when we ask: What is the *meaning* that Luke intends? Jesus is not so much going up into outer space as going into the omnipresent God. Here we have something "higher" than a space event. While some New Testament writers use "exaltation" language, saying that Jesus was "exalted" or "raised up" into heaven (Philippians 2:9; 1 Timothy 3:16; Hebrews 7:26), Luke's presentation of early preaching about the ascension of Jesus is quite dramatic.

Each style of literature has to be judged according to its own intention and form. So what was the intention of the early preaching we find in Luke?

The Church offers us excellent pointers in the second readings chosen for the feast of the Ascension:

- In Year A (and also, optionally, in Years B and C) we have Ephesians 1:17-23. This tells us that Christ is now with each and every community scattered over the earth. The risen and ascended Lord is not localised now in one place such as Jerusalem.
- In Year B we have an alternative reading in Ephesians 4:1-13. The death that was supposed to put an end to the influence of Jesus has (such irony!) itself been made captive… and all are now given gifts for the building up of the universal Church.
- In Year C we are offered Hebrews 9:24-28 and 10:19-23. The Jerusalem Temple is no longer needed since Christ is our *universal* high priest, interceding now in heaven for everyone everywhere – something that we stress in every Mass, especially at the end of the preface when we are invited to join our liturgy with the liturgy of heaven: "May our voices blend with theirs as we sing…"

So the ascension drama is teaching us a crucial lesson: the risen Jesus is now *our* Christ, no longer localised in Judea and Galilee, but with us here and throughout all of time. The ascension is outwards rather than upwards. So we need not waste time looking upwards at the clouds. Rather we should "get stuck in", doing kingdom work as witnesses. At the ascension, the disciples are formally commissioned to be "witnesses", a word that in Greek is *martures*. We don't need to know much Greek to realise that this word can be translated as "martyrs" – though it also looks like "matures", and maybe there's food for thought there too! Being a mature "witness" today, either in the marketplace or, often with more difficulty, in our own families, can require us to put our heads into the stocks and take a bit of flack!

To be a "martyr" today will require us to re-energise our batteries. We can do this in union with that heavenly liturgy going on now in heaven with Jesus and in the communion of saints, all taking place for us in time and space, but also beyond the barriers of space and time. Maybe that's what the ascension is about!

THE FOURTH GOSPEL

We have seen that each Gospel writer has painted his own portrait of Jesus. Mark has told us that you cannot understand Jesus unless you see him as a suffering Messiah. For Matthew, Jesus was the great teacher. For Luke, the mission of Jesus was not just for his own Jewish people but for everyone, reaching out "to the ends of the earth". The writer of the Fourth Gospel similarly has his own perspective: Jesus is the life-giving "Word made flesh".

"In the beginning"

The writer starts his Gospel using the same words as Genesis. He seems to say, "The real beginning was even before creation, when the Word was 'with God'": "In the beginning was the Word… and the Word became flesh… and we have seen his glory."

The divinity of Jesus

It is not difficult to see how the early Church struggled to understand the divinity of Jesus. In Paul's letter to the Romans, around AD 58, he wrote that Jesus was declared to be God's Son *at the resurrection*: "the gospel concerning his Son, who was descended from David according to the flesh and was declared to be Son of God… by *resurrection from the dead*" (Romans 1:3-4).

So, naturally, people could ask: "But was he Son of God *before* this resurrection?" Well, we then find in Mark (around AD 65–75) that he was indeed God's Son before this, at his baptism: "And just as he was coming up out of the water, he saw the heavens torn apart and the Spirit descending like a dove on him. And a voice came from heaven, 'You are my Son, the Beloved; with you I am well pleased'" (Mark 1:10-11).

But the questioner could continue: "What about *before* his baptism? Was he God's Son before this event?" And so we find Matthew and Luke (around AD 80–90) telling us that he was Son of God *at his very conception*.

A totally new question now arises: Did this special person exist in some way *even before he was conceived?* And we find the answer at the start of the Fourth Gospel: Yes! "In the beginning was the Word… He was in the beginning with God."

The "teacher from God"

We only have to dip into this great Gospel to find how different it is in style from the other Gospels. Jesus often speaks in long noble speeches or discourses, as befits a divine teacher. He also describes himself using the divine name ("I AM"), the name revealed by God to Moses at the burning bush (Exodus 3:14):

- I AM the bread of life (6:35. 51);
- the light of the world (8:12);
- the sheep gate (10:7. 9);
- the good shepherd (10:11. 14);
- the resurrection and the life (11:25);
- the way, the truth and the life (14:6);
- the true vine (15:1. 5).

The writer lets us know that God is truly present in Jesus in these ways.

Jesus similarly challenges the hearers on other occasions: "you will die in your sins unless you believe that *I am* he" (8:24); "When you have *lifted up* the Son of Man [a Greek pun on being 'strung up' on the gibbet of the cross], then you will realise that *I am* he" (8:28). This is a most powerful statement: when you look at the crucified one, then you will see what God ("I AM") is really like! He goes on: "Before Abraham was, *I am*" (8:58).

In 18:5, when the soldiers and police announce that they are seeking Jesus to arrest him, he says, "I am he." While this means at one level simply "I am he", yet there is a deeper level: the soldiers fall to the ground in fear as they hear the divine name present in Jesus.

The whole Gospel is written "so that you may come to believe" (20:31). In a sense the entire Gospel is one great trial scene, in which the writer puts forward his evidence in a very systematic way. He even puts God the Father into the witness box! His list of witnesses includes:

- the Baptist (1:7-8. 15. 32. 34; 3:26; 5:33);
- the Samaritan woman (4:39);
- the Samaritans (4:42);
- Jesus himself (8:18; 18:37);
- the "works" of Jesus (5:36; 10:25);
- the Father (5:37; 8:18);
- the Hebrew scriptures (5:39);
- the Paraclete (15:26);
- the disciples (15:27);
- and the beloved disciple (21:24).
- Thomas sums it all up when he says, "My Lord and my God!" (20:28).

It can be useful to have a simple "map" to guide us through this profound Gospel. One way is to imagine a great pendulum, sweeping down from on high to its lowest level and then sweeping back up again in one great curve. The diagram below tries to show this. In the beginning the Word is "with God". Then, over a period of twelve chapters (covering three years), this Word sweeps down to "his own people", presenting them with seven great signs pointing to his identity. His own people refuse to receive him. In chapter 12 "some Greeks", foreigners, come seeking Jesus. And only then does Jesus exclaim: "The hour has come for the Son of Man to be glorified" (12:23).

This is the great turning point, when, like the upward ongoing sweep of the pendulum, Jesus is about to return, through his glorious passion, back into the bosom of his Father. His cry from the cross will be a great shout of victory, "It is finished" (19:30), as he breathes out his Spirit on the infant Church, the new creation, the woman (the new Eve) and the beloved disciple at the foot of the cross.

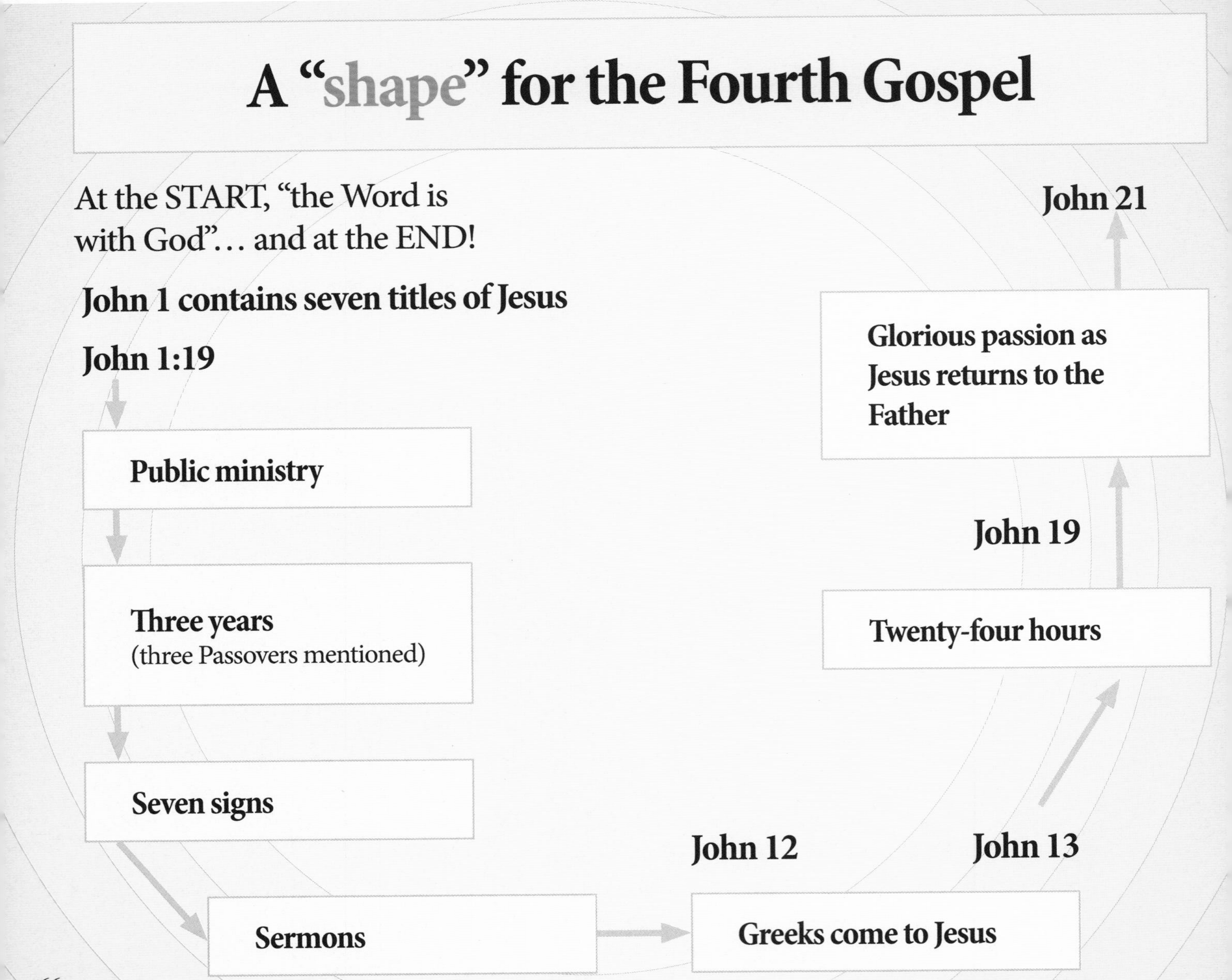

A "shape" for the Fourth Gospel

At the START, "the Word is with God"… and at the END!

John 1 contains seven titles of Jesus

John 1:19

John 21

Glorious passion as Jesus returns to the Father

Public ministry

Three years
(three Passovers mentioned)

John 19

Twenty-four hours

Seven signs

John 12   **John 13**

Sermons   **Greeks come to Jesus**

The beloved disciple

This is a title given to someone who appears only towards the end of the Gospel. He seems to have lived in or around Jerusalem and he appears for the first time at 13:23 at the Last Supper. He is a friend of the high priest (18:16). Some have suggested that he was Lazarus, whom Martha and Mary described to Jesus as "he whom you love" (11:3); and the Jews also said, "See how he loved him!" (11:36) when they saw Jesus weeping at the tomb of Lazarus. Associated with this could be the rumour that the beloved disciple might not die (21:23), presumably because Lazarus had died once already before Jesus raised him. Anyway, the beloved disciple had a lot to do with the handing on of *at least* chapter 21 of the Gospel (21:24).

We do not know who was the final editor of the Gospel that is now in our official sacred scriptures. We do know that it was eventually published, not by the eyewitnesses themselves but by disciples of the beloved disciple after his death (21:24). There is no reason to doubt the tradition that the *authority* behind the Gospel was John the fisherman, the "son of thunder", the son of Zebedee. But the *author* of our final text, a writer of polished Greek, is an unknown disciple.

Conclusion

This very rich Gospel seems to present Jesus as we would have seen him in his lifetime, if only we had looked upon him with the new eyes of faith that we now have as a result of our faith in the resurrection.

And each one of us is called to be a loving disciple of this great "teacher from God", the victorious Son of God, the Word of God made flesh in order to bring us abundant life.

What is our answer when Jesus asks us, as he did Peter, "Do you love me?"

Graphical summary of the Gospels

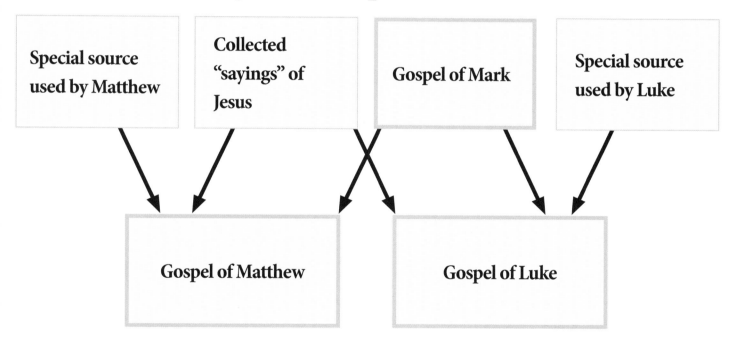

Special source used by Matthew	Collected "sayings" of Jesus	Gospel of Mark	Special source used by Luke

Gospel of Matthew	Gospel of Luke

MARK'S GOSPEL:
for persecuted Christians. Rome.
c. AD 65–75

MATTHEW'S GOSPEL:
for Jewish / Gentile Christians. Antioch?
c. AD 80–90

LUKE'S GOSPEL:
for Gentile Christians. Antioch?
c. AD 80–85

THE FOURTH GOSPEL:
theological reflection on Christ. Ephesus?
c. AD 90–100

All dates very approximate. (Add or subtract ten years.)

THE RESURRECTION: AN INVITATION TO HAND ON FAITH

If it didn't happen, you wouldn't be reading this. No resurrection – no Church, and no *Your Bible*! Simple.

St Paul put it this way: "If Christ has not been raised, then our proclamation has been in vain and your faith has been in vain" (1 Corinthians 15:14).

Paul, our earliest writer on the risen Lord, was sure *that* something happened. But no writer in the New Testament ever says *how* it happened. And our scientific age just wants to ask that "how?" question.

Yet *what* happened – the foundation of our faith – is that, in the resurrection of Jesus, God broke through our barriers of space and time and revealed the real presence of the Lord Jesus in a way that was new, yet continuous with the Jesus his disciples had met in his earthly ministry.

No one saw Jesus being raised as they had seen Lazarus being resuscitated. Lazarus would finally die like the rest of us, but the risen Lord was raised in a way that was totally new for us to understand or describe.

Regarding the "how?" question, Paul used the image of a seed dying and being transformed into new life:

"But someone will ask, 'How are the dead raised? With what kind of body do they come?' Fool! What you sow does not come to life unless it dies. And as for what you sow, you do not sow the body that is to be, but a bare seed, perhaps of wheat or of some other grain… What is sown is perishable, what is raised is imperishable. It is sown in dishonour, it is raised in glory. It is sown in weakness, it is raised in power. It is sown a physical body, it is raised a spiritual body." (1 Corinthians 15:35-37. 42-44)

He is struggling to find words to express the change from weakness to power, from a physical body to a spiritual body.

But Paul knows that Jesus is risen, because he has met the Lord in the mystical experience on the Damascus road. And he has also heard the witnesses before him:

"For I handed on to you as of first importance what I in turn had received: that Christ died for our sins in accordance with the scriptures, and that he was buried, and that he was raised on the third day in accordance with the scriptures, and that he appeared to Cephas, then to the twelve. Then he appeared to more than five hundred brothers and sisters at one time, most of whom are still alive, though some have died. Then he appeared to James, then to all the apostles. Last of all, as to someone untimely born, he appeared also to me." (1 Corinthians 15:3-8)

Years later, when both Paul and Peter are dead, we find the story of the resurrection being written down in narrative form. This is a form of literature designed to express a truth.

Our very existence as Church arises from the fact of resurrection

The Gospel writers were not interested in how Jesus was raised. Their primary purpose was to call people to believe in the risen presence of Jesus and to encourage those who already believed to remain strong in their faith.

Nevertheless, people today still line up the four Gospels and ask:

- Was it several women or only one (as in John) who came to the tomb?
- Why did they come – to anoint the body or to inspect the tomb (as in Matthew)?
- Was the stone already rolled back or did an angel do it in the women's presence (again as in Matthew)?
- Who was there: one man, two men, one angel or two angels?
- Were these men or angels inside or outside the tomb, standing or sitting?
- Did the women tell the other disciples or keep silent (as Mark says)?
- To whom did Jesus first appear: the women (Matthew 28:9-10), Mary Magdalene (John 20:14-17) or Simon Peter (Luke 24:34)?

Such questions are not the evangelists' questions. The "honest truth" is the fact of resurrection, which they struggled to present for their own communities without the aid of tape recorders or videos.

The Gospels do tell us how this totally unexpected event affected the early witnesses. They were not gullible fools. This was not the resuscitation of a corpse that was readily recognisable like that of Lazarus.

For some it took time for the new reality to sink in:

- some doubted (Matthew 28:17);
- Mary Magdalene thought the risen Jesus was the gardener (John 20:15);
- the disciples on the road to Emmaus only recognised the risen Lord at the breaking of bread (Luke 24:31).

Thomas and us

In the upper room, Jesus says to Thomas: "Give me your hand!" (John 20:27). This is a wonderful invitation to trust the risen Lord – and then "give him a hand" in the work of kingdom building.

In our prayer, we still need these Gospel pictures and stories that pinpoint different ways of appreciating the real event of the first Easter. We need to reflect, to get into the picture, using our imagination in order to absorb the reality of the event that continues to break through from beyond space and time into our present existence.

"Thomas answered him, 'My Lord and my God!' Jesus said to him, 'Have you believed because you have seen me? Blessed are those who have not seen and yet have come to believe.'" (John 20:28-29)

This is our faith. Here is my hand!

A CLOSER LOOK AT JESUS

The letter to the Hebrews tells us that Jesus was like us in every respect except sin (2:17-18; 4:15). So he had to grow in body, knowledge and experience (Luke 2:52).

He probably lived for a time in a one-room, mud-brick house. His mother would prepare the usual light breakfast – a snack with milk, melted butter and perhaps fish, or eggs and some olives (see John 21:12-15) – while the family would have lunch at midday and the main meal in the evening.

Bread was made from cereal grains like wheat, millet or barley and could be eaten with raw leeks, cucumbers or cheese. The frying pan was used a lot, sometimes to make flour cakes.

Beans were the food of those who were poor, being baked or boiled in oil with garlic, or soaked and eaten with butter and pepper. Fish and eggs were eaten, and sometimes meat from lambs, goats, pigeons or chickens when available. Melons, grapes, dates, nuts, oranges and lemons provided dessert, with watered wine accompanying the meal. The household would sleep by unrolling their mats around the fireplace.

At the age of six or seven, a boy like Jesus would be taken to the local synagogue school for basic education until he was ready for his bar mitzvah, at which he publicly became a Jewish adult. At other times he would learn his father's trade – perhaps, in Jesus' case, working on a building site in nearby Sepphoris or Tiberias.

This was the sort of human background we can imagine for Jesus before his public ministry.

We know that he experienced a special awareness of who he was when he heard God's voice at his baptism in the Jordan. We know how he called followers, taught about God's kingdom in parables, healed many and eventually was executed and raised from the dead.

Getting to know Jesus better

In his farewell prayer at the Last Supper, Jesus solemnly prayed for us to get to know him better: "This is eternal life, that they may know you, the only true God, and Jesus Christ whom you have sent" (John 17:3).

G.K. Chesterton once encouraged his fellow Catholics to keep growing in knowledge of God through posing adult questions. He mused that it would be very strange if the more we knew about God then the less we would see the great love of God. The same could be said of our adult growth in knowledge and love of Jesus.

It is easy to duck questions by saying: "Jesus was God, he had divine knowledge and that's that!" But great theologians like St Thomas Aquinas urged us to take the humanity of Jesus seriously:

"Divine knowledge cannot be an act of the human soul of Jesus; it belongs to another nature. *The divine knowledge of the second person of the Trinity could not function in a human mind.* A human mind works through concepts and ideas; it thinks. Divine knowledge is of a different nature: it does not need to put concepts together and make judgements; it is immediate and intimate and thorough. This kind of knowledge could not function within the limitations of a human mind." (*Summa Theologica*, III q.9)

Obviously, a good place to look for the human Jesus, "one who in every respect has been tested as we are, yet without sin" (Hebrews 4:15), would be to see what the Gospel writers gave us, from AD 65 to 100. But it is reasonable to peep behind the Gospels and explore reverently the sort of world in which Jesus grew up, in the so-called "hidden years".

A few questions may help us to relate to Jesus as he "increased in wisdom and in years, and in divine and human favour" (Luke 2:52):

1. What language did Jesus speak?

Scholars are divided on this: Greek? Aramaic? Hebrew? The young Jesus grew up in Nazareth, an unimportant village in Galilee. Here he would have spoken the common language of Aramaic, with a "northern" accent, using the dialect of Galilean western Aramaic. (In terms of our own culture, he would not have a posh "BBC" delivery!) He would have heard Hebrew in the synagogue readings. Hebrew was the conservative "religious" language; Aramaic translations called Targums were commonly used to supplement the lectionary readings of the Hebrew Bible texts. Joseph may well have sent him to learn Hebrew in the synagogue school as a bright "firstborn son" who was subject to his parents (Luke 2:51). Anyway, Jesus' reading of Isaiah in Luke 4:16-20 and his habit of debating with both scribes and Pharisees could suggest some knowledge of biblical Hebrew… or did he use the Aramaic translations, the Targums?

Greek: The knowledge of Greek varied from class to social class. But the demands of trade and the need to converse with the larger world would have led Jesus, with Joseph, to pick up enough Greek phrases to strike bargains and write receipts. Later on in his ministry, we may wonder if he had an interpreter for Greek speakers in his audience? Perhaps someone with a Greek name, like Andrew or Philip (John 12:22)? We know that Jesus taught ordinary Palestinian Jews. He became, in time, an Aramaic teacher.

2. Was Jesus illiterate? Did he learn to read and write?

The Gospel evidence is doubtful about this. John 8:1-11 (about the woman caught in adultery and Jesus writing in the sand) is not found in the earliest manuscripts of this Gospel, though the story is found in some manuscripts of Luke. Some scholars suggest that it is a second-century story on the treatment of sinners. But it is now in our sacred canon of scripture. The great scripture scholar Fr Raymond Brown, in his commentary on John's Gospel, suggested that Jesus was just doodling on the ground to distance himself from the accusers. But even a few written words in the sand say little about Jesus' literacy.

On the other hand, we find in John 7:15 Jews marvelling about Jesus: "How does this man have such learning, when he has never been taught [with us in Jerusalem]?"

Furthermore, Luke 4:16 tells us about Jesus reading Isaiah 61:1-2 in the Nazareth synagogue. And we learn elsewhere of his debates with the educated laymen, the Pharisees. It is likely, therefore, that Jesus could read some biblical Hebrew.

3. Was Jesus a *poor* carpenter?

With regard to poverty, those who were poor or dispossessed were at the bottom of the ladder; Joseph, although not wealthy, was somewhere in the middle economically: he would have led a precarious existence at the mercy of weather, market prices, inflation, grasping rulers, wars and heavy taxes (religious and civil).

The reputation for Jesus being a "woodworker" hangs by a single thread. Mark has the neighbours saying, "Is not this the carpenter, the son of Mary and brother of James and Joses and Judas and Simon, and are not his sisters here with us?" (6:3). So we get the word "carpenter" from half a verse of only one Gospel. Matthew, perhaps out of reverence, changes Mark, making Jesus only the "the carpenter's *son*" (13:55). The Greek word they both use is *tekton*, which is really a general builder. Jesus may well have worked with Joseph on a building site in the nearby town of Sepphoris, three or four miles from Nazareth, which Herod Antipas was rebuilding as his capital, until he moved to a new capital, Tiberias, built around AD 26. But the Gospels never mention this Gentile town, only the traditional Jewish villages: Nazareth, Cana, Capernaum, Chorazin.

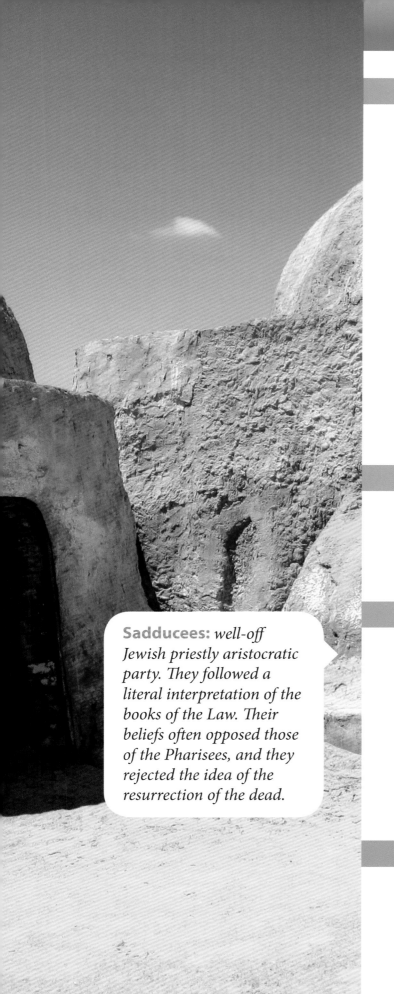

4. Did Jesus have brothers and sisters?

The word "family" was understood differently from today: it included the extended community of cousins, aunts and uncles. Jesus' break with this left deep scars: the family thought he was "mad" (Mark 3:21; see also 3:31-35; 6:1-6). Jesus was wary of their motives. We read in John 7:2-10:

"Now the Jewish festival of Booths was near. So his brothers said to him, 'Leave here and go to Judea so that your disciples also may see the works you are doing; for no one who wants to be widely known acts in secret. If you do these things, show yourself to the world.' (For not even his brothers believed in him.) Jesus said to them, 'My time has not yet come, but your time is always here. The world cannot hate you, but it hates me because I testify against it that its works are evil. Go to the festival yourselves. I am not going to this festival, for my time has not yet fully come.' After saying this, he remained in Galilee. But after his brothers had gone to the festival, then he also went, not publicly but as it were in secret."

It leaves us wondering if Jesus had a rough time growing up with his younger family members.

5. Was Jesus married?

It's been suggested that since Jesus was a rabbi he must have been married. The Gospels tell us that Jesus related to many named characters. Surely if he had been married his wife would have been mentioned? Jesus chose to live the unusual path of celibacy.

6. Was Jesus a layman?

> **Sadducees:** *well-off Jewish priestly aristocratic party. They followed a literal interpretation of the books of the Law. Their beliefs often opposed those of the Pharisees, and they rejected the idea of the resurrection of the dead.*

The priests of Jesus' time were **Sadducees**. We can be quite sure, from the fierce debates Jesus had with the Sadducees and their involvement in his execution, that Jesus was not one of them! Yes, Jesus was a layman. He did not offer priestly sacrifice in the Temple.

Many years later, after the Temple had been destroyed by the Romans, Christians thought of Jesus as offering a new kind of sacrifice, the sacrifice of his life on the cross. In that sense Jesus could be seen as a priest. In fact the letter to the Hebrews reflects on him being our new high priest (9:11-14).

7. Who do *you* say I am?

In conclusion, our prayer each day with Jesus, now the risen Lord, can hopefully be enriched in the knowledge that he was "tested as we are, yet without sin" (Hebrews 4:15), that he grew up, and "increased in wisdom and in years" (Luke 2:52), like most of us, in very ordinary circumstances, without any religious power base. Nevertheless, he made an enormous difference by responding to his Father's call to bring all to the knowledge of God's saving love. Who do we say he is, and where is the risen Lord calling us today?

A closer look at Jesus
THE BEATITUDES

"Be glad the day you have sorrow…" It is common to hear this verse, from the hymn "Be still, and know I am with you", sung at funerals. Many find the words distinctly uncomfortable. How can the relatives and friends of the deceased "be glad" when they are grieving, often very deeply? Did Jesus actually say that when he gave us the Beatitudes? Perhaps we need to go back to our Gospels and check.

Luke gives us four Beatitudes, which are then balanced by four Woes (Luke 6:20-26). Matthew expands on these and gives us eight Beatitudes (or nine if you include verse 11, which is different in that this one is addressed to "you"; Matthew 5:1-12). In both Gospels the words of Jesus are given in Greek. But Jesus would have addressed his friends in the local language, Aramaic. Obviously, what we now have is a translation into English from a translation into Greek from the original Aramaic words used by Jesus. And, even then, our English translations differ. Some give us *"Happy* are you poor", and so on, while others have *"Blessed…"* The hymn mentioned above, with poetic licence, uses the words "Be glad…" So what did Jesus really say?

The Aramaic word he probably used sounds like "ashray". It is a term of congratulation, recommendation and encouragement. Basically it means, "Hang on in there: you're doing well; you're getting through it. My heart is with you in your struggle!" How weak are our English efforts when this becomes "Blessed", or "Happy"! When Jesus sees people who are poor and grieving, his attitude, which should be ours too, is "I am with you in support. I see the good in you. If I may, I would like to congratulate you on the way you are coping!"

Matthew, who puts this teaching into the Sermon on the Mount, sees the Beatitudes as the basic attitude for the followers of Jesus.

1.   "Poor in spirit": Matthew recognises that, for his flock of Christians, the Beatitudes of the kingdom require inner dispositions. He points the focus away from the negative (poverty, distress and hunger) towards the very positive, towards attitudes the Christians need to profess to become "blessed" – detachment and humility.

2.   "Those who mourn" may include those in Matthew's church whose suffering is caused by the bodily absence of Jesus as they struggle in faith and hope for the building of the kingdom, in spite of the contempt or indifference of the world around.

3.   "The meek" are the gentle, who, according to Psalm 37:11, "shall inherit the land". The meek surrender themselves totally to God, taking Jesus' yoke upon them, for he is "meek and humble of heart". Active non-violence was witnessed to by people like Hélder Câmara, Martin Luther King and Gandhi. For them the "land" should be a space in which people can be themselves and completely free, a "God-place", a "kingdom-of-God-place". Now, if possible!

4.   "Those who hunger and thirst for righteousness": righteousness refers to a good relationship with God. We need to seek first this kingdom and this righteousness (Matthew 6:33). Such is our be-attitude here, the "attitude" we should "be" experiencing.

5.   "The merciful": mentioned only here in the New Testament (apart from Hebrews 2:17, where it is used of Christ). The original Old Testament word, *chesed*, doesn't mean feeling sorry for someone, but it does mean being able to get inside another's skin. The unmerciful on the other hand insist on their own rights. So try to get inside the other person and see things from his or her point of view. God's mercy is always a gift; our mercy is a spontaneous response to this free gift of God.

6.   "The pure in heart": much of Israel's law was directed towards ritual purity before approaching the Temple etc. The prophets, of course, were against ritualism: see, for example, Hosea 6:6; Amos 5:21-27; Jeremiah 7:3-7. To be "pure in heart" does not mean to be sinless, and certainly should not be primarily interpreted in terms of chastity. The "pure in heart" are those who are upright, whose motives are unmixed, whose minds are utterly sincere, who are completely single-minded, whose interests are undivided.

7.   "The peacemakers": the Greek word *eirenopoios* is only found here in the New Testament. It is associated with the Hebrew word "shalom" and is very rich in content: it seems to come from a root that means "complete", intact. Peace is not the opposite of war but of everything that disturbs the well-being and prosperity of individuals and communities. Such peace needs justice. Peacemakers are not the same as peacekeepers – the latter often use force of arms! Kingdom values are at the heart of the Beatitudes: social justice, progress and peace for all peoples. Like the kingdom, peace is both a gift and a task.

8.   "Those who are persecuted for righteousness' sake" are the reviled: "for theirs is the kingdom of heaven" is an echo of Matthew 5:3, rounding off things. Jesus' followers can expect three kinds of bad treatment: revilement, persecution and calumny. We may well ask, "So what has changed?"

A CHECK-UP WITH THE BEATITUDES

Just as a car needs a service from time to time, so may we occasionally feel the need for a personal check-up, taking time for some quiet reflection on our way of life. It may be at the turn of the year, a significant birthday or perhaps in our preparation for the sacrament of reconciliation. The following prayer may start us off as an examination of conscience.

Jesus says to me, "Blessed are the poor in spirit, for theirs is the kingdom of heaven."
I say to Jesus, "Lord, when I am puffed up with self-importance, remind me of my basic inner poverty. Help me to make this space uncluttered and open for you to enter with your kingdom values."

Jesus says to me, "Blessed are those who mourn, for they will be comforted."
I say to Jesus, "When I am grumpy and hard to get on with, when I tend to live in the past, harbouring regrets, or when I really need support through dark times, remind me that the Holy Spirit is near me as Comforter and Advocate."

Jesus says to me, "Blessed are the meek, for they will inherit the earth."
I say to Jesus, "When I am pushy, self-seeking and over-ambitious, remind me to pause and act with respect for the feelings of those I meet, so that we may work in harmony for the kingdom."

Jesus says to me, "Blessed are those who hunger and thirst for justice, for they will be filled."
I say to Jesus, "When the emptiness of my selfishness gives way in me to a real hunger for a fairer and more just society, fill me with courage and energy to reach out in practical action outside my safe shell."

Jesus says to me, "Blessed are the merciful, for they will receive mercy."
I say to Jesus, "Show me the obvious and the deeply hidden grudges within me, and then inspire and free me with your own forgiveness to be a forgiving person myself. Help me to be slow to condemn, and less resentful or touchy in future."

Jesus says to me, "Blessed are the pure in heart, for they will see God."
I say to Jesus, "I would love to see the divine presence around me, but I often become tied up with the devious designs of my heart. Inspire me now so that I may imitate your sincerity and simplicity of heart and see God around and within me."

Jesus says to me, "Blessed are the peacemakers, for they will be called children of God."
I say to Jesus, "Where do I need to make peace? In my family? Neighbourhood? Church community? Point me, Lord, to one specific area where you are calling me to be a peacemaker and to act as a true child of God."

Jesus says to me, "Blessed are those who are persecuted for the sake of justice, for the kingdom of heaven is theirs."
I say to Jesus, "Lord, those who try to build up a just society often meet with backbiting and sneering, or are singled out for painful isolation and harassment. Inspire me with courage, so that, like you, I may persevere in standing up for what is right (and avoid becoming a persecutor myself)."

Do it yourself! Every town these days has its DIY sales outlet. Television abounds with "makeovers": lots of instant fixes for your house, your garden or even your face! Sadly, those of us who have attempted DIY may have met with the less encouraging response, "If you need a job well done, then go to the professionals!"

When it comes to the spiritual life and the subject of prayer then, from time to time, our DIY efforts can also meet with some frustration. We can seek help from the many books on the subject; we may look for a "professional", a spiritual director to help us on the way as we try to sustain a lively, relevant practice of prayer. These guides will normally point us in the direction of the one great "professional" – Jesus.

We may hesitate when Jesus is put before us as a model of the praying person. After all, we may think, he was God: it was easy for him! If we think like that, then maybe we need to take more seriously words from the letter to the Hebrews: "we do not have a high priest who is unable to sympathize with our weaknesses, but we have one who in every respect has been tested as we are, yet without sin" (4:15).

There is also much for us to learn about the humanity of Jesus from the great hymn in Paul's letter to the Philippians: "though he was in the form of God, [Jesus] did not regard equality with God as something to be exploited, but emptied himself, taking the form of a slave, being born in human likeness" (2:6-7). With Jesus being "emptied" and born like us we can with profit look at his prayer experience for help with our own human struggles in prayer.

Jesus praying

Luke in particular shows us that Jesus prayed on so many occasions.

At his baptism: "Now when all the people were baptized, and when Jesus also had been baptized and was praying, the heaven was opened, and the Holy Spirit descended upon him in bodily form like a dove. And a voice came from heaven, 'You are my Son, the Beloved; with you I am well pleased'" (3:21-22). Is this a *prayer of dedication* as he seeks his vocation in life? A *prayer of listening* perhaps?

Before choosing the twelve: "Now during those days he went out to the mountain to pray; and he spent the night in prayer to God. And when day came, he called his disciples and chose twelve of them, whom he also named apostles" (6:12-13). Is this a *prayer of wondering or discernment*?

When he was challenged about his identity: "Once when Jesus was praying alone, with only the disciples near him, he asked them, 'Who do the crowds say that I am?'" (9:18). Is this a *prayer for courage*, to say and do things that are not going to be popular?

When prayer led to the transfiguration: "Now about eight days after these sayings Jesus took with him Peter and John and James, and went up on the mountain to pray. And while he was praying, the appearance of his face changed, and his clothes became dazzling white. Suddenly they saw two men,

Moses and Elijah, talking to him" (9:28-30). Is this a *prayer of contemplation*?

He prayed to strengthen Peter: "Simon, Simon, listen! Satan has demanded to sift all of you like wheat, but I have prayed for you that your own faith may not fail; and you, when once you have turned back, strengthen your brothers" (22:31-32). Is this a *prayer of petition*?

Jesus prayed on the cross: "Then Jesus said, 'Father, forgive them; for they do not know what they are doing'" (23:34). Is this a *prayer of intercession*?

He prayed in his last breath: "Then Jesus, crying with a loud voice, said, 'Father, into your hands I commend my spirit.' Having said this, he breathed his last" (23:46). Is this a *prayer of trust*?

In all of these occasions we find the true "professional" person of prayer. So it is no wonder that his disciples came to him for help when they found him wrapped in prayer. He gave them a *prayer of community*: "He was praying in a certain place, and after he had finished, one of his disciples said to him, 'Lord, teach us to pray, as John taught his disciples.' He said to them, 'When you pray, say: Father, hallowed be your name. Your kingdom come…'" (11:1-2).

This prayer leaves us with a job to do: we are to be people who forgive. What does that mean today? Yes, we are asked to forgive our neighbour. But, as we shall see, we are also to get involved in the removal of debts – prayer for the remission of debts comes from the mouth of Jesus himself, towards the end of the Our Father: "And forgive us our sins, for we ourselves forgive everyone indebted to us" (11:4).

Our Father…

The "Lord's Prayer" appears in Matthew (6:9-15) and Luke (11:2-4) in slightly differing forms. Luke's version is short. Matthew's is longer and is the one we are accustomed to in the liturgy.

It has been said that the number of Christians who could recite Luke's version could fit into a phone box. Yet the core is the same as Matthew's.

Both address God as "Father" (Matthew's community version has "Our Father") and both pray for the remission of debts.

The New Testament manuscripts use the Greek work *aphiemi* – often translated as "forgive". But behind the word is the Jewish meaning, "remit" – put things back again, wipe the slate clean.

In Matthew 18:21-35 we are particularly asked as a church to be forgiving… not seven times, but seventy-seven times! As church people we are to be in the forefront of promoting remission or forgiveness. Why? Simply because we have been forgiven by God!

No offence against us can even remotely compare with the immeasurable amount we ourselves have been forgiven. Jesus gives the parable of the servant who has received remission from a debt of 10,000 talents (Matthew 18:24). Here the largest Greek numeral is combined with the highest unit of currency. God's forgiveness is beyond our wildest imaginings.

It is possible to trivialise this teaching on our duty of forgiveness by making an erroneous use of Jesus' address to "Abba". We could think that God is our "Daddy", our "Papa", and so we needn't be concerned too much.

But recent scholarship would stress that "Abba" does *not* equal the baby word "Daddy". Adults use it. In the mouth of the adult Jesus it means "my own dear Father".

It is the direct, trusting and unaffected address of someone who is dependent on an all-powerful and loving Father. It is far from trivial. But it is shockingly new in the sense that Jesus invites his followers to address God as their own dear Father too.

The whole prayer is in the plural. It has two sections: firstly as a community we make two petitions in what is known as the passive voice – that the Father's name be sanctified and that his rule will extend throughout our less-than-heavenly world. In Jewish usage the use of the passive voice meant that it was mainly up to God to do this!

But then secondly there are four "us" prayers. We say give us bread, remit our debt, deliver us from evil and lead us not into temptation.

The last one can be puzzling. How could God "lead us into temptation" anyway? The early Christian writer Tertullian said that we could read it as "let us not be led into temptation". It may be useful to remember that a big temptation, then as now, is to turn to apostasy, to deny our faith and its public responsibilities when put to the test.

Matthew stresses: "If you forgive others their trespasses, your heavenly Father will also forgive you; but if you do not forgive others, neither will your Father forgive your trespasses" (6:14-15). That's a tough condition!

When it comes to the liturgy, Matthew again reminds us: "When you are offering your gift at the altar, if you remember that your brother or sister has something against you, leave your gift there before the altar and go; first

be reconciled to your brother or sister, and then come and offer your gift" (5:23-24).

It comes as no surprise, then, that the Our Father is the opening prayer of the communion rite of our Mass. Our prayer for remission is followed by the sign of peace and the great sacrament of communion with Christ and with one another in Christ.

It is so easy to think that all of this is just a matter for "my soul and Jesus". We can be sorry for personal sin and forget about our responsibility for social sin – the sin "out there" for which I am in part responsible, either by the way I relate to politicians in power or by my silence.

The Lord's Prayer puts demands on our lives. The "dear loving Father" we address is also the lover of all who are crushed by debt. Our words of prayer are important but not enough. They must not be empty.

Jesus says, "Do not heap up empty phrases as the Gentiles do; for they think that they will be heard because of their many words" (Matthew 6:7).

Thank God, our churches are indeed at the forefront of the movement for international debt remission. Let each of us too be counted as we walk in generous solidarity with them.

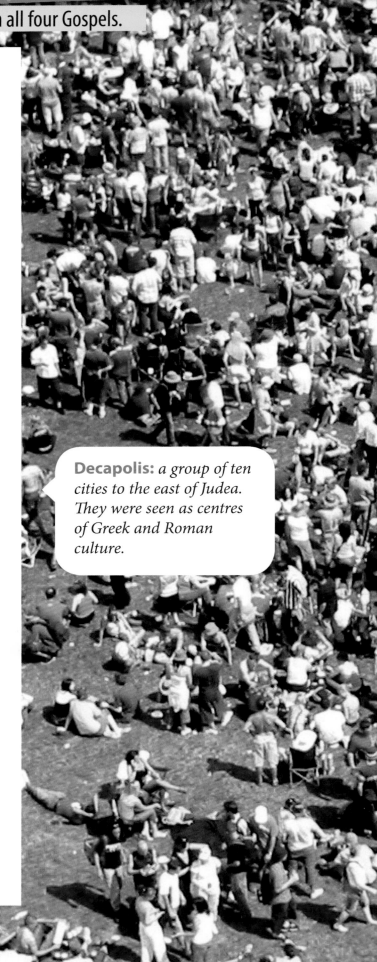

The story of Jesus feeding the crowd occurs in all four Gospels.

In Mark, the earliest Gospel, we find it in two forms: Jesus feeds five thousand people with five loaves and two fish (6:30-44); and later we are told of four thousand being fed with seven loaves and a few fish (8:1-10).

The first account is set in a mainly *Jewish* territory. The Galilean countryside reminds us of God providing manna to feed the Hebrews in the wide open spaces of the desert. Mark's wilderness is, however, green with the spring rains.

The disciples want to turn away the crowds, but Jesus takes the little resources they have so that their poverty is blessed; their little is shared and found to be thoroughly satisfying to the crowd. A poor resource is no excuse for turning folks away. Shared resources in the presence of Jesus can be totally transformed.

Mark's words describing what Jesus did are Eucharistic in tone: "He *took*… he *blessed*… he *broke*… he *gave*." In our Mass, these actions are repeated – at the preparation of gifts Christ's minister *takes* the bread, then *blesses* it at the consecration, *breaks* it at the "Lamb of God" and *gives* it to us in communion.

The Jewish character of Mark's first account is further emphasised by the collection of leftovers in twelve baskets, symbolising the twelve tribes of Israel.

Mark's second feeding story is situated in *Gentile* territory, in the old **Decapolis** region. It comes after Jesus has been confronted by a Gentile woman (7:24-30). She is pleading for the cure of her daughter: "Sir, even the dogs under the table eat the children's crumbs." Jesus is moved to minister to this non-Jewish woman and her daughter.

The Old Testament book of Deuteronomy saw the goal ahead of the Exodus people to consist of overcoming seven pagan nations (7:1). In the New Testament seven is also a sign of completeness and universality. Now Jesus *takes* seven loaves of bread; he then gives *thanks*, which in the Greek of Mark's Gospel is *eucharistesas*. Literally, Jesus "eucharists". Then he *breaks* and *gives* the bread.

"They ate and were filled; and they took up the broken pieces left over, seven baskets full" (8:8). Here Mark uses a word for a basket that is different from the first account. The word now is *spuridas*, which means a large basket: each one was big enough to hold a human being. The nourishment of the Gentile mission is no small task!

These two feeding stories seem to be a prophetic preparation for the meal at the Last Supper (14:22-25). Here is the fulfilment: the bread is now Jesus' body. The wine is important too: Jesus says it is "my blood of the covenant, which is poured out for many".

Decapolis: *a group of ten cities to the east of Judea. They were seen as centres of Greek and Roman culture.*

Clearly at the Last Supper there is now a deep sacrificial dimension to this. Jesus' violent death is being offered for "many" (not just for the few). The blood of the covenant recalls the action of Moses, who took sacrificial blood, then sprinkled half on the altar, symbolising God's side of the new relationship, and the rest on the people, making them one blood, one life with God (Exodus 24:8). That's what Jesus' sacrificial blood does.

Each of these feeding stories also reflects the weakness and frailty of the disciples. After the feeding of the five thousand, the disciples "did not understand about the loaves, but their hearts were hardened" (6:52). After the second feeding, Jesus had to ask: "Do you still not perceive or understand? Are your hearts hardened?" (8:17).

The Last Supper has the institution of the Eucharist preceded by the betrayal of Judas. It is followed by Jesus' prophecy about the denial of Peter. Indeed, "All of them deserted him and fled" (14:50). An unhappy pair of brackets for the Eucharist! Yet none of this puts Jesus off. He emphatically assures us that, having gone through with it all, he "will drink of the fruit of the vine… new in the kingdom of God" (14:25).

We can rejoice in the way God gradually reveals the gift of the Eucharist through the Old and New Testaments. The prophet Ezekiel was asked by God to eat the scrolls of scripture and make them part of himself (Ezekiel 2:8). We are doubly privileged to share Jesus in the liturgy of the word and also in sacrament. Both are real presences of God.

Let us continue to deepen our appreciation and enjoyment of these two real gifts each day.

Surely Luke's second volume is one of the most exciting books of the entire Bible. It gives us a thrilling account of the early Church's missionary outreach "to the ends of the earth".

It also supplies us with important details of its pastoral activity: we are introduced to the prayer life of the early communities; we find them trying to share their possessions; there is also some evidence of what we would now call a "sacramental" celebration of baptism and Eucharist. We learn of the early attempts towards church organisation, involving "teachers" and "elders" and "prophets". We also find truly dramatic accounts of the death of Stephen, and of Peter's fierce treatment of Ananias and his wife Sapphira when they tried to deceive their community.

But all of this follows from the foundation event, the tremendous outpouring of the Holy Spirit at Pentecost. Given that Luke mentions God's Spirit some seventy times in Acts, this book has been called "the Gospel of the Holy Spirit".

Sources

Since both Luke's Gospel and Acts would not have fitted into the length of a single scroll of writing material, Acts became a second volume for Luke's story. It probably became separated from his Gospel halfway through the second century, when there was an attempt to bind together all four of the Gospels into a single book.

Where did Luke get all his material for this second instalment? Firstly he would have referred to a Greek translation of the Jewish scriptures, since this was commonly used in the Greek-speaking Church. He may also have received some written documents, such as the account of the martyrdom of Stephen. Then there would have been traditions from the primitive Jerusalem community, which he uses in the first five chapters. He may have had to hand someone's biography of Peter (9:32 – 11:18), and perhaps one of Philip the evangelist (8:4-40), whom Luke actually met in Caesarea (21:8). In addition, Luke seems to have composed a travel diary as he moved around with Paul, for he frequently uses the word "we" in these passages. All of these sources were arranged by Luke in a grand plan of universal salvation, from Jerusalem "to the ends of the earth".

Luke's purpose

Luke wanted his community to be encouraged to face the future by looking at its past. That's not a bad idea for us today. In spite of dungeon, fire and sword (literally!), the Spirit in the Church from the very beginning gave, and still gives, hope for the future. We can summarise the great story in this way:

1:12 – 8:3 The Spirit gives birth and growth to the community in Jerusalem.

8:4 – 9:31 In spite of persecution, the Spirit expands the community into Judea and Samaria.

9:32 – 15:35 Gentiles now find a home in the Church through the Spirit working in Peter and Cornelius, in Barnabas and Saul, and in the Council of Jerusalem (c. AD 49) under James the relative of Jesus (not the apostle James – he had been martyred earlier, see Acts 12:2).

15:36 – 21:14 The Spirit leads Paul overseas on several missions to the Gentiles.

21:15 – 26:32 Paul returns to Jerusalem, where he witnesses to the resurrection and is arrested.

27:1 – 28:31 "We" (says Luke) sail to Rome, and Paul teaches for two years in rented lodging. "He… welcomed all who came to him, proclaiming the kingdom of God and teaching about the Lord Jesus Christ with all boldness and without hindrance" (28:31).

Peter and Paul

Luke is at pains to show how similar these great men are.

	Peter	Paul
Both heal a man lame from birth	3:2-8	14:8-10
Both pronounce judgement	5:1-5	13:11
Both perform miracles in an unusual way	5:15	19:12
Both exercise a ministry of healing	9:34	28:8
Both have a Gentile convert from a noble family	10:1	13:12
Both are led by a vision to minister to Gentiles	10:9-20	22:17-21
Both are reverenced	10:25	16:29
Both experience the support of the Holy Spirit	10:44	19:6
Both are rescued from prison	12:7	16:26

Yet it is Peter who is named first in the list of apostles (1:13); Peter makes the foundation speeches in Jerusalem both before and at Pentecost (1:15 and 2:14); it is Peter who, moved by the Spirit, baptises the first Gentile, Cornelius, ignoring the Jewish food laws (10:1-48). But Peter makes his final appearance only halfway through Acts, at the Council of Jerusalem (15:7) – and that is the last we hear of him! For the final thirteen chapters Luke's interest focuses on Paul. Perhaps Luke is pleading on behalf of the new boy, Paul: "You know how great Peter is; well, Paul is just like him, so accept him as OK. He is truly one of us in spite of his early days of persecution."

Luke as the "spin" doctor?

There are many scholars who distrust Acts as a source of historical information. They say that you only have to look at Paul's own letters to see how different they are in their descriptions of Paul's life and his theology from what we see in Acts. For example, Acts 22:3 tells us that Paul was brought to Jerusalem as a youth and educated there at the feet of Gamaliel (a famous Jewish teacher who taught there during the time of Jesus). If Paul spent his youth in Jerusalem, is it not likely that he would have come across Jesus? Yet Paul never mentions any encounter with the public ministry of Jesus.

Secondly, according to Paul's own letter to the Galatians, he went to Jerusalem after his conversion only after three years, and again after around fourteen years (Galatians 1:17-18; 2:1). But according to Acts, Paul visited Jerusalem at least five times, one of them being immediately after his conversion (9:26-29) and another later, when he brought famine relief to the city along with Barnabas (11:29-30). Critics suggest that Luke intended to paint an idealised picture of the early Church by playing down tensions there and in particular by showing a calmer, less rebellious character for Paul than we find in Galatians.

Scholars of the last couple of centuries were also sceptical about Acts because of the frequency of the miracles found there. They assumed the prejudice that miracles are simply unscientific and don't happen. More modern critics are far less sceptical in view of the attested healings associated with prayer today.

Real tensions

But Luke does give us a hint of the tensions in the early Church. We see James presiding in Jerusalem. From other sources we learn that this James had gained a reputation for being very ascetic. He was Jewish in his piety, praying and worshipping as a Jew, while believing in Jesus, whom he had seen as the risen Lord.

In contrast we find other followers of Jesus, known as the Hellenists, who had little place for traditional Jewish restrictions and who particularly spoke out strongly against the Temple with its worship and central control. Stephen was one of these, and in his great speech he implied that the Temple had become an idol! This was enough to bring about his execution, with its profound effect on Saul, or Paul as he became known later.

Reading between the lines, we see that Stephen's burial was arranged by "devout men" (8:2) rather than by "the church". These Hellenists were then persecuted and scattered, "preaching the Good News", while the apostles (with James) seem to have remained silent in the background and free from persecution. In time, however, James himself was martyred (in AD 62). The Jerusalem church disappeared from history with the destruction of Jerusalem in AD 70. Did it die of conservatism?

Tell us more, Luke!

It seems a pity that we have so little information about what the other apostles did. It would have been especially interesting to learn in our scriptures about what happened to Peter.

We know that Paul wrote to the church in Rome before he intended to visit it. He mentions in Romans 16 a huge list of Christians living there (but not a word about Peter). Who founded the church there? Did it arise from "visitors from Rome" who were in Jerusalem at Pentecost and went back home as converts, setting up the church there (Acts 2:10)?

Luke doesn't even suggest that Peter worked outside Palestine. He is not interested in our Western twenty-first-century questions! Nevertheless, Luke has shown that Paul follows Peter in so many ways, as we have noted above. Luke is most helpful in continually stressing that the energy of the Holy Spirit is at work in every missionary expansion, the Spirit that is the common bond of unity, holding all things together in dynamism. It is the Spirit that keeps us very much on the move today, reaching out to all nations, even to us at the ends of the earth.

Thank you,
Luke!

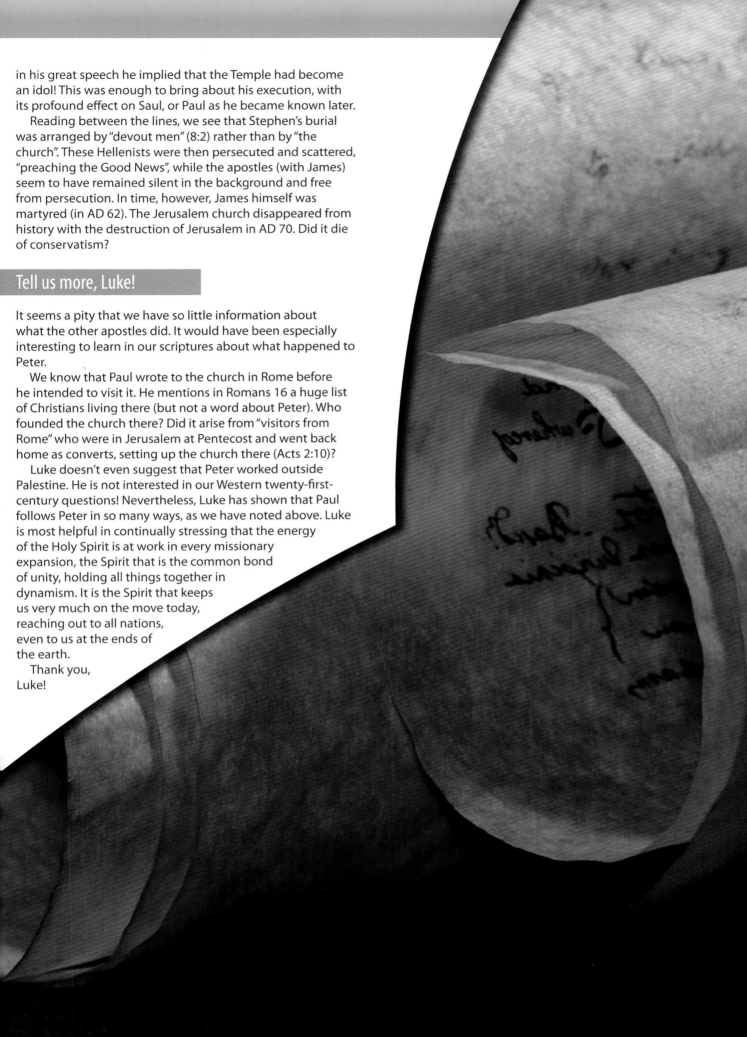

Peter is a complex character in the New Testament. We read how Jesus made him the rock on which the Church would be built: "you are Peter, and on this rock I will build my church" (Matthew 16:18).

But we're also told how Paul – calling Peter by his Aramaic name, Cephas – roundly reprimanded him: "But when Cephas came to Antioch I opposed him to his face…" (Galatians 2:11).

Yet Paul, in his first letter to the Corinthians, does put Peter at the head of the list of the witnesses to the resurrection (15:5). And in the same letter he gives a list of persons who have a right to support for themselves and their families, singling out Peter (9:5). So Paul certainly seems to recognise the universal authority of Peter.

Peter in the Gospels

To get a fuller picture of Peter, it makes sense to see how he is portrayed in the Gospel communities.

Mark

Mark, the earliest Gospel, opens with the call of Simon Peter and Andrew (1:16-20), and ends with the angel's message to "the disciples and Peter" (16:7). Many scholars would say that Mark got his information mainly from Peter, the man who converted him (1 Peter 5:13). Perhaps this is the reason Mark gives us such a blunt, honest picture of Peter – a picture many of us find so attractive.

Jesus stays in Peter's house along with the mother of Peter's wife (1:29-30). Peter is present at the raising of Jairus' daughter (5:37). Peter is the one who speaks for the group and confesses Jesus as Messiah, only to be strongly rebuked by Jesus: "Get behind me, Satan!" (8:27-33). He has to learn that Jesus is to be a *suffering* Messiah! At the transfiguration, Peter is confused, and dithers about setting up three tents for Jesus, Moses and Elijah (9:5). When Peter asks Jesus about rewards, he is told to expect persecution (10:28-31). Later, he boasts loyally that he will never be scandalised by Jesus (14:29); and soon he is found fast asleep as Jesus prays in Gethsemane. Although three of them are sleeping, it is Peter who is addressed by Jesus (14:37). Then, after Peter has denied Jesus three times (14:66-72), the angel of the resurrection brings a message to "his disciples and Peter" (16:7). Of course Jesus will take him back!

Luke

Luke, as we would expect, is much gentler towards Peter. At Caesarea Philippi he omits Peter's protest and the rebuke of Jesus. He simply attaches teaching on the need for every disciple to take up the cross daily (9:20-27).

Before the passion, Jesus prays for Peter: "Satan has demanded to sift all of you like wheat, but I have prayed for you [Simon] that your own faith may not fail; and you, when once you have turned back, strengthen your brothers" (22:31-32). Luke recasts Mark's "even though all will become deserters, I will not", by making Peter say, "Lord, I am ready to go with you to prison and to death!" (22:33). This points to Peter's later imprisonment and death. Luke omits from Mark that all the disciples made a similar protest, gently moving them off stage while highlighting the fate of Peter. Similarly, on the Mount of Olives, in Mark's account Jesus rebukes Peter specifically for sleeping, and then rebukes the whole group. But in gentle Luke there is an excuse: they had been sleeping "because of grief" (22:45).

In Luke's passion account, Peter's denial is softened. Instead of saying, as in Mark, "he began to curse, and he swore an oath, 'I do not know this man you are talking about'", Luke has "'Man, I do not know what you are talking about!' … The Lord turned and looked at Peter… And he went out and wept bitterly" (Mark 14:71; Luke 22:60-62). Luke finally echoes a tradition that Peter was the first to see the risen Lord: "The Lord has risen indeed, and he has appeared to Simon!" (24:34).

Matthew

Matthew's Gospel is the only one to mention church. Jesus gives Peter the power of the keys, calling him the foundation rock (16:13-20). Yet a few verses later, the rock has become a stumbling-block! Matthew sharpens Jesus' rebuke from Mark's account.

Then in Matthew the community also gets the power of binding and loosing as a disciplinary tool (18:18). The context for this is forgiveness: "How often should I forgive?" (18:21).

John

In the Fourth Gospel (John), written after Peter's death, we find a contrast between Peter and the beloved disciple. It is almost a "one-upmanship" picture that is presented from John's community: the beloved disciple is the one to be admired for fidelity. Seven clear points of "one-upmanship" occur:

1. At the Last Supper, Peter features significantly in the feet-washing scene as one who has to follow Jesus' example of service (13:3-15). But he cannot speak directly to Jesus about Judas and has to go through the beloved disciple as an intermediary (13:23-24).

2. In the other Gospels, Peter is the only one of the twelve to follow Jesus into the high priest's courtyard. But in John he cannot do this until the beloved disciple arranges for his admittance (18:15-16).

3. In the other Gospels, Peter eventually abandons Jesus and no male follower goes to the cross. In John, the beloved disciple is faithful and is found near it to the end (19:26).

4. In John, Jesus makes the beloved disciple his brother by making Mary John's mother too (19:26-27).

5. In New Testament circles, Peter is often the first to see the risen Lord (1 Corinthians 15:5; Luke 24:34). But in John, while both Peter and the beloved disciple run to the tomb, it is the beloved disciple who is first to believe, and he does so without "seeing" Jesus (20:8).

6. When both have been fishing and they see Jesus on the shore, Peter does not believe until the beloved disciple tells him: "It is the Lord!" (21:7).

7. Finally, this Gospel shows us that love brings Peter closer to the Lord much more than any status of being the most important apostle. In chapter 21, Peter is appointed to feed the sheep only after three times confessing his love. Peter has first and foremost to be a loving disciple.

Acts and onwards

When we come to Acts we find that, at Pentecost, there were Jews "from Rome" who were converted and who presumably went back home and set up the Christian community there around AD 33.

We do not know when Peter arrived in Rome. The New Testament doesn't mention this. Acts says he was still in Jerusalem for the Council there around AD 49.

But in the first letter of the church leader Clement to the Corinthians, written from Rome at the turn of the century, we read of the martyrdom of Peter and Paul:

"Through envy and jealousy, the greatest and most righteous pillars [of the Church] have been persecuted and put to death. Let us set before our eyes the illustrious apostles: Peter, through unrighteous envy, endured not one or two, but numerous labours, and when he had at length suffered martyrdom, departed to the place of glory due to him.

"Also owing to envy, Paul obtained the reward of patient endurance, after being seven times thrown into captivity, compelled to flee, and stoned. After preaching both in the east and west, he gained the illustrious reputation due to his faith, having taught righteousness to the whole world, and come to the extreme limit of the west, and suffered martyrdom under the prefects. Thus was he removed from the world, and went into the holy place, having proved himself a striking example of patience."

In the final decades of the first century, we find there are letters written in *Peter's* name to the furthest corners of the Roman Empire, exhorting Christians to be steadfast in the face of persecution, and urging those in Asia Minor to be faithful to the message of faith they have received from the missionary work of *Paul*.

There is obvious approval of Paul in these epistles of Peter, where we find pastoral responsibility *in Peter's name* being directed to the universal Christian Church.

The rocky journey continues!

Near the end of the New Testament writings we come across what are called the catholic letters. These seven writings, composed towards the end of the first century, consist of three attributed to John, one each to James and Jude, and two in the name of Peter.

Outside the New Testament, there is an extraordinary amount of writing made in the name of Peter. We find the *Gospel of Peter*, as well as three apocalypses of Peter and several "Acts" of Peter. Not many of us are familiar with the story of Peter and the smoked tuna, but it exists, in chapter 5 of the *Acts of Peter*:

"Peter turned round and saw a smoked tunny-fish hanging in a window. He took it and said to the people, 'If you now see this swimming in the water like a fish, will you be able to believe in him whom I preach?' Now there was a fishpond nearby…"

You can guess the rest of the story! It is not surprising, then, that early on the Church put aside such weird popular tales and established a canon, or rule of inspired scripture that was used in the community's liturgical readings. Our two letters from Peter are, of course, treasured members of the canon of scripture.

Although Peter is thought to have been martyred around AD 67, these letters may have been written in his name after Peter's death by the secretary Silvanus (1 Peter 5:12), who was probably also Paul's companion known as "Silas" (Acts 15:22).

No one knows when Peter first came to Rome. When Paul wrote his letter to the Roman Christian community there around AD 58, he sent greetings to some twenty-eight named individuals, but there is no mention of Peter among these (Romans 16). What is important, however, is that, shortly after the death of Peter and Paul, we find a letter written from the church in Rome, in the name of Peter. This style of writing, known as pseudepigraphy, is a recognised convention of the time. We might call it forgery, but that would be misleading. The thinking was: "This is what Peter would say to you now if he were alive today." It is sent with the full authority of the church in Rome to the remotest outposts of the Roman Empire in Asia Minor, where new Christians are undergoing persecution. Rome's pastoral authority is not in doubt by this time. And Peter's leadership is clearly recognised and used.

One of the interesting sources that Silvanus seems to have employed is a baptismal homily from Peter. We find it in 1 Peter 1:3 – 4:11. Here is a truly beautiful exhortation to the newly baptised, urging them to holiness, calling them "a royal priesthood" (2:9). They are to be conscious of their dignity, for our God has no favourites (1:17). Women are to be recognised as equal heirs – an astonishing claim at a time when inheritance was through male dominance only (3:7). This equality must lead to mutual respect and love. Why? So that they can pray together as equals in the liturgy! The homily encourages them furthermore to be respectful citizens, obedient slaves (where appropriate), considerate spouses and loving members of the community. Love for one another and for Christ is at the heart of everything: "Although you have not seen him, you love him" (1:8). Like Jesus before them, they will experience suffering. In fact suffering is mentioned more in this letter than in any other New Testament writing. Yet they are to hang on in there, keeping their minds "serious… for the sake of your prayers" (4:7). They are to be confident as they reach out to others, always having their answers ready to explain their faith. No wonder the Church uses this letter today in its Eastertide liturgy!

The second letter, also written in sophisticated, polished Greek, warns against false teachings. It wants to draw back into the fold those people who were distorting what they thought they had learned from Paul's letters. Anyone today who has ploughed through some of Paul's letters and found them to be somewhat obscure may laugh at finding in this letter one of the great understatements in the whole Bible: the writer says of the letters of "our beloved brother Paul" that "there are some things in them hard to understand" (3:16). But the important point is that "the ignorant and unstable twist [these things] to their own destruction, as *they do the other scriptures*". The writer of Peter's second letter has already stressed that the interpretation of scripture is not an individual matter (1:20). But here, amazingly, he is treating Paul's letters as *scripture* – like "the other scriptures"!

Perhaps we could now spend some prayer time reflecting on the sacred text of the baptismal homily in 1 Peter 1:3 – 4:11. Its profound richness can still powerfully reach out to us today from these Roman roots of our Church. We have surely come a long way from the smoked tuna! Or have we?

Let us look now at Paul's experience of the risen Lord and the effect this had on his life and letters.

It is not Paul who tells us about the road to Damascus – this comes in Luke's Acts of the Apostles, written probably in the 80s.

So what does Paul himself say about his encounter with the Lord? He describes it on only one important occasion, and even there the words seem to fail him. We find it in the second letter to the Corinthians.

Paul seems so frustrated with his opponents that he lets slip what was a most profound personal experience. Speaking of himself (in the style of a rabbi, perhaps), he writes:

"I know a person in Christ who fourteen years ago was caught up to the third heaven – whether in the body or out of the body I do not know; God knows. And I know that such a person – whether in the body or out of the body I do not know; God knows – was caught up into Paradise and heard things that are not to be told, that no mortal is permitted to repeat." (2 Corinthians 12:2-4)

Paul's rapture has allowed him to meet Christ in glory: not the Jesus of Nazareth (whom he would not recognise since he probably had never met Jesus) but the *cosmic* Christ, the Lord of creation and time. This vision is so powerful it is beyond human words. Paul sums it up in the phrase "in Christ". He sees profoundly that "in *Christ* God was reconciling the world to himself" (2 Corinthians 5:19).

When Paul finally wrote about his vision of the cosmic Christ he also curiously mentioned the "thorn" he was given:

"To keep me from being too elated, a thorn was given to me in the flesh, a messenger of Satan to torment me, to keep me from being too elated. Three times I appealed to the Lord about this, that it would leave me, but he said to me, 'My grace is sufficient for you, for power is made perfect in weakness.' So, I will boast all the more gladly of my weaknesses, so that the power of Christ may dwell in me. Therefore I am content with weaknesses, insults, hardships, persecutions, and calamities for the sake of Christ; for whenever I am weak, then I am strong." (2 Corinthians 12:7-10)

Scholars have made guesses at the nature of this "thorn". Maybe Paul had a physical deformity or a disability of some sort. He had a weakness in speech, perhaps a stammer (1 Corinthians 2:1; 2 Corinthians 10:9-10; 11:1); he may have had problems with his eyes (Galatians 4:13-15; Acts 23:5); perhaps he suffered from malaria or epilepsy; perhaps the thorn was a persistent critic – "a thorn in his side", as we might say today.

While *all* of these may have afflicted him, surely one overriding thorn was his human inability to express adequately his profound experience of the cosmic Christ: the one who:

"is the image of the invisible God, the firstborn of all creation; for in him all things in heaven and on earth were created, things visible and invisible, whether thrones or dominions or rulers or powers – all things have been created through him and for him. He himself is before all things, and in him all things hold together. He is the head of the body, the church; he is the beginning, the firstborn from the dead, so that he might come to have first place in everything. For in him all the fullness of God was pleased to dwell." (Colossians 1:15-19)

Great words, but a pale reflection of the reality of the experience!

As a result of this meeting with the risen Lord, Paul frequently uses the phrase "in Christ" to express his theology:

1. "...*in Christ* Jesus you are all children of God through faith. As many of you as were baptized *into Christ* have clothed yourselves with Christ. There is no longer Jew or Greek, there is no longer slave or free, there is no longer male and female; for all of you are one *in Christ* Jesus." (Galatians 3:26-28)

2. "...as all die in Adam, so all will be made alive *in Christ*." (1 Corinthians 15:22)

3. "Do you not know that all of us who have been baptized *into Christ* Jesus were baptized into his death? ... if we have been united with him in a death like his, we will certainly be united with him in a resurrection like his... if we have died with Christ, we believe that we will also live with him... you also must consider yourselves dead to sin and alive to God *in Christ* Jesus." (Romans 6:3-11)

4. "...we, who are many, are one body *in Christ*, and individually we are members one of another." (Romans 12:5)

5. "For I am convinced that neither death nor life... nor anything else in all creation, will be able to separate us from the love of God *in Christ* Jesus our Lord." (Romans 8:37)

Paul sums it up when he says: "For to me, living is Christ" (Philippians 1:21). And he tells us: "we are the aroma of Christ" (2 Corinthians 2:15) – better than any perfume or aftershave! When we're around, folk should sense Christ's presence. Wow!

PAUL: APOSTLE TO THE GENTILES

It's not often you get a laugh when dealing with St Paul! Here is how a late-second-century writer described him in a work called the *Acts of Paul*: Paul was "a man of short stature, with a bald head and bowed legs, with eyebrows meeting and a crooked nose, yet in good state of body and full of friendliness".

The laugh is that the modern reader can so easily misinterpret what the author is saying: in the writings of those days people of short stature were thought to be quicker and brighter than tall individuals, because blood moved faster through a short body than through a tall person; the meeting of eyebrows was at that time thought to be a sign of beauty; a hooked nose indicated that the person was of royal bearing and generous-hearted; bowed legs showed that someone had his or her feet firmly balanced on the ground and was therefore highly practical; and (here's a consolation for some of us) baldness was a sign of great humanity, for, it was argued, you never found mere animals going bald!

It may not be important for us to know what Paul actually looked like, but from his many letters and Luke's Acts of the Apostles we find a character who was indeed mentally quick, who dealt realistically with new problems as they arose, and who, judging from the huge list of friends he had (see, for example, Romans 16), was a person of great humanity.

Convert

Most of us know about the conversion of Paul on the road to Damascus (where his oft-mentioned horse is purely a figment of later imagination). There he met the risen Lord Jesus in the presence of a blinding light. Thereafter his life was radically transformed.

He had been born into a Jewish family of the tribe of Benjamin, circumcised on the eighth day following; he tells us he was "blameless" under the law, living as a Pharisee (Philippians 3:5-6), zealous for the traditions of his ancestors. His first language was Greek; his education probably took place in the lively intellectual centre of Tarsus, a thriving cosmopolitan city on the eastern Mediterranean.

Acts tells us that he was brought to Jerusalem at an early stage to study under the great intellectual Rabbi Gamaliel (Acts 22:3; 26:4). Like many of today's students, Paul had to support himself in practical ways: his father had taught him the trade of leather-working. On the Damascus road he met someone who simply said, "I am Jesus, whom you are persecuting." Paul did not abandon his education after his conversion; equipped with a first-class Greek and Jewish education and a powerful new faith, Paul was ready to take on the world and to keep on learning from his new experiences as he did so.

After his conversion he spent time in the deserts of Arabia before returning to Damascus and preaching there (Galatians 1:17; Acts 9:20). Fourteen years later, along with Barnabas, he went to

Jerusalem and became recognised as apostle to the Gentiles. Faced with those whom he referred to as "acknowledged pillars" of the church, he tells us in Galatians 2 that he was not afraid to challenge Peter to his face! While he was reconciled with the apostles in Jerusalem, spies who doubted his orthodoxy still continued to hound Paul behind his back. This didn't put off Paul in the least, though, being Paul, he does let off steam against them in very impolite ways (Galatians 6:13). He seems to say, "I wish when you were circumcised that the knife had slipped!"

Traveller

There was a time when "the journeys of Paul" formed a section of religious education schemes. Students may have learned of his three great journeys. But often the geographical facts got in the way of the human reality.

Paul mentions the dangers in 2 Corinthians 11:26. Before the days of credit cards and cheque books, travellers had to take their money with them. Many brigands were on the prowl as the result of poverty and greed. Travellers would band themselves into groups, often carrying cudgels for their own protection. This meant that their arrival at a village was met with suspicion. The Roman poet Ovid described how villagers "were in such alarm that they unchained a pack of mastiffs which they kept as watchdogs, very savage beasts… and set them about us with shouts, halloos and discordant cries" (***Metamorphoses*** 8:17).

There were also enormous packs of wolves. "We were warned that the road we wished to take was strewn with half-eaten corpses and clean-picked skeletons… and that we should travel only in broad daylight – the higher the sun the milder the wolves" (*Metamorphoses* 8:15).

Inns were spaced about 35 km apart and even they were far from secure: thieving was widespread while guests were sleeping in the communal room, or if the travellers had left their luggage behind them while bathing or taking refreshment. And yet Paul, with a comfortable living assured to him as an educated Pharisee, travelled thousands of hazardous miles, urged on simply by the love of Christ.

Metamorphoses:
A poem about creation, in fifteen books, completed by the Roman poet Ovid in AD 8.

Builder of communities

From Paul's letters we know something about the communities set up or supported by him; but our knowledge is limited. Often he is writing to clarify teaching he has been asked about, or to correct behaviour that was reported to him. For example, it is only in 1 Corinthians 11 that he mentions the Eucharist. But he does so because there are drunks in that community! No doubt there were celebrations of the Lord's Supper in other communities, but he doesn't need to mention them in his letters.

Paul's letters presuppose that missionaries and their teaching have gone before him, so we cannot expect to find in them systematic or exhaustive presentations of doctrine. Yet his letters contain deep ways of appreciating the saving power of the crucified and risen Lord.

The last we hear about Paul in scripture is when Luke tells us about him being taken to Rome. He does not tell us how he died. A late second-century or third-century work (*Acts of Paul*) tells us that he was beheaded there, probably during the reign of Nero… before a single Gospel had been written. Paul's Gospel was his life of outstanding mission, teaching, and witness to the crucified and risen Lord, who justifies us by the free gift of his love.

The following is a creative exercise. We begin with a picture of Paul with his two feet on the ground. Imagine you are with Paul as he moves along a city street on his travels. Everything he passes reminds him of our life in Christ. If you have time, look up the Pauline references beside each location. Like Paul, try to "Let the same mind be in you that was in Christ Jesus" (Philippians 2:5), seeing the things around you with a new dimension, with an awareness of their deeper significance. And if you want to read more of Paul's letters, a good place to continue the journey would be with his letter to the Galatians.

Pawn Shop
Gal 3:13; 4:5;
Rom 3:24

Fruit Shop
1 Cor 9:7;
Rom 7:4-5

Slave Market
Rom 7:14;
1 Cor 7:21

Temple and Sacrificing
1 Cor 2; 6:19; 8:10;
Rom 3:25

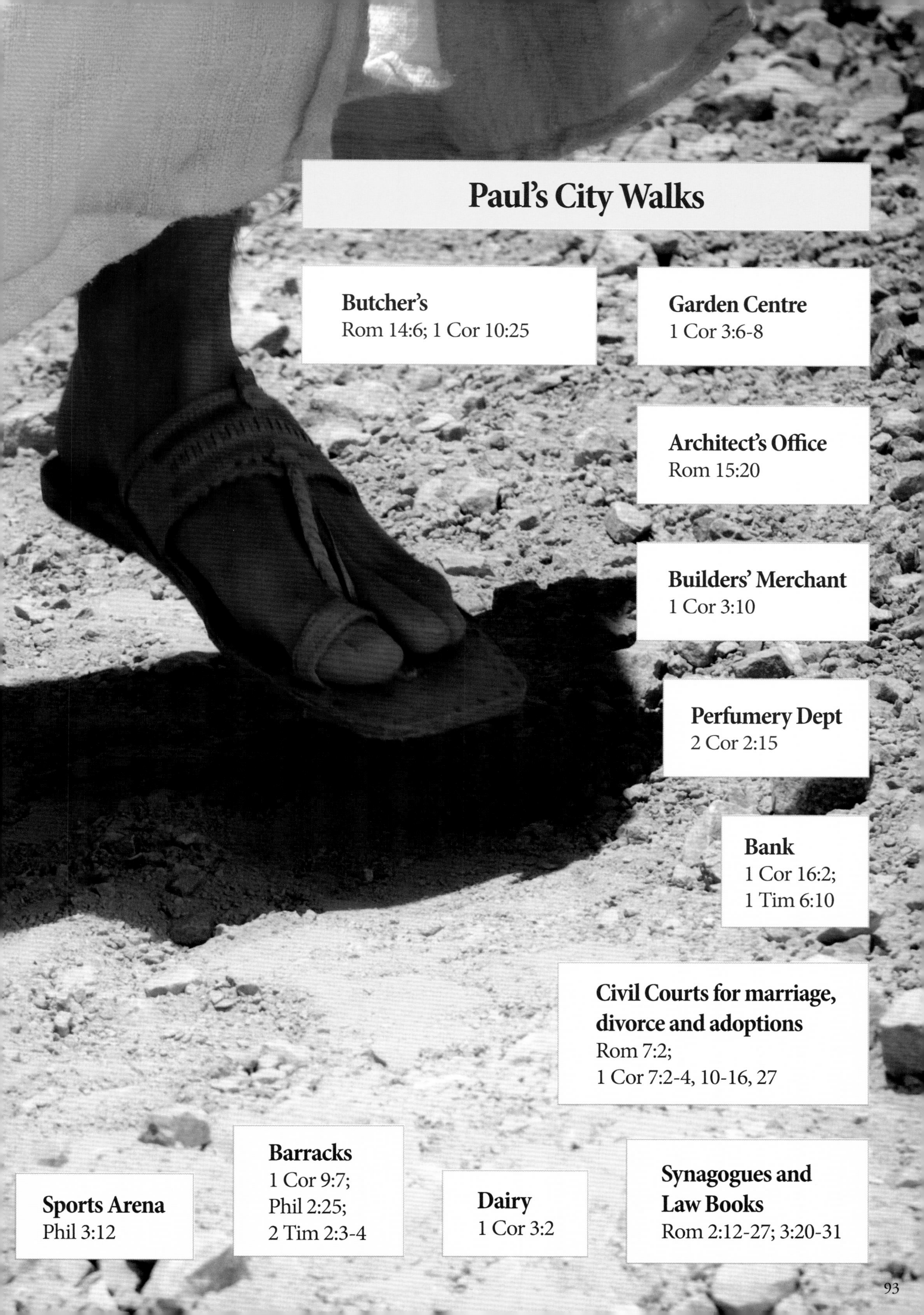

Paul's City Walks

Butcher's
Rom 14:6; 1 Cor 10:25

Garden Centre
1 Cor 3:6-8

Architect's Office
Rom 15:20

Builders' Merchant
1 Cor 3:10

Perfumery Dept
2 Cor 2:15

Bank
1 Cor 16:2;
1 Tim 6:10

Civil Courts for marriage, divorce and adoptions
Rom 7:2;
1 Cor 7:2-4, 10-16, 27

Barracks
1 Cor 9:7;
Phil 2:25;
2 Tim 2:3-4

Sports Arena
Phil 3:12

Dairy
1 Cor 3:2

Synagogues and Law Books
Rom 2:12-27; 3:20-31

PAUL IN ACTION: GALATIANS

Roughly three hundred years before Jesus, Celtic tribes from around central Europe set off on their travels. Some went in a northerly direction, but others battled their way east into Asia Minor.

These tribal Gallic Asians – Asians from Gaul – or "Galatians" are described by Greek and Roman historians like Polybius and Livy as "barbarians, devoid of any Greek culture, fighting naked, without any order or tactics, armed with swords and large wooden or wicker shields. Their pastoral life, long remote from cities, helped them to preserve their native customs and language for many years."

As they slowly settled down amid the local people, and as Jewish colonists were imported into Asia Minor, an elaborate religious system began to reign over the country.

Especially among those who were uneducated, there arose two features of religious practice:

- a superstitious devotion to a multitude of rules and regulations;
- an unthinking loyal obedience to the directions of the local pagan priests.

The Christian mission had a lot to deal with when the Good News was brought to Galatia. Paul had his work cut out for him.

As time went on, many Christian converts had fallen back into sectarian loyalties associated with the person who had first evangelised them. Paul found also that many of them had reabsorbed from the surrounding culture a reliance on gaining "merit" through the performance of pious practices instead of accepting on faith the free gift of God's love, God's grace.

Paul's letter to the Galatians is written against certain individuals who had disturbed the faith of the converts. Paul had preached that Christ had set aside the Law; he had argued that Gentiles did not need to be circumcised into Judaism before becoming Christians. But his critics insisted that Paul was a heretic rather than a real apostle.

So Paul starts off his letter in an angry defence of his authority: "the gospel that was proclaimed by me is not of human origin... but I received it through a revelation of Jesus Christ" (1:11-12).

He goes on to demand, "You foolish Galatians! Who has bewitched you? ... Did you receive the Spirit by doing the works of the law? ... Are you so foolish?" (3:1-3).

Paul stresses that there are to be no sectarian prejudices in the churches of Galatia: "You are *all* children of God through faith" (3:26). *All* are baptised into Christ, so "There is no longer Jew or Greek, there is no longer slave or free, there is no longer male and female; for all of you are one in Christ Jesus" (3:28).

He warns that there must be no turning back into superstitious practices: "How can you want to be enslaved to them again? You are observing special days, and months, and seasons, and years. I am afraid that my work for you may have been wasted" (4:10). "Christ has set us free. Stand firm, therefore, and do not submit again to a yoke of slavery" (5:1). "In Christ Jesus neither circumcision nor uncircumcision counts for anything; the only thing that counts is *faith working through love*" (5:6).

Paul calls for unity: "Let us not become conceited, competing against one other and envying one another" (5:26).

All of this may make us wonder if perhaps there is still lurking in us, as there was in Paul's "Gallic Asians", a slight tendency towards sectarian loyalties, ignoring the good in others. Perhaps too we may be tempted to imagine that our pious practices should somehow force God to reward us with "merit", when in fact God owes us nothing – all is grace, the free gift of God's unconditional love in Jesus.

A life of devotion and pious practices is excellent, but it has to be a response of love on our part. In both of these areas Paul urges us to "live by the Spirit" (5:16). And the fruits of the Spirit are "love, joy, peace, patience, kindness, generosity, faithfulness, gentleness, and self-control" (5:22).

Our good works are to be a response to God's love, not a condition for it.

Holidays are good for bookshops. Whether going off on a break or on a retreat, people look for "a good read" to take with them.

Taking a fairly unfamiliar book of scripture as a travelling companion is recommended as food for the mind and the heart. The letter to the Ephesians, taken in bite-sized portions, offers rich fare.

Ephesus is in one of today's popular holiday destinations, Turkey. But there is more to recommend it than simply a holiday hot spot.

There are several interesting questions surrounding this letter. While most modern Bibles say it is written to the church community in Ephesus, the best of the early manuscripts don't indicate this specific destination – they omit the phrase "in Ephesus".

It may have been a circular letter, dispatched to various communities. It doesn't tackle local church problems or issues, but covers matters of doctrine important for everyone.

On the question of authorship, St Paul's hand is definitely at work, but there are sufficient discrepancies between this and his seven undisputed letters also to suggest another style or hand at work:

- The sentences are very long, with lots of subordinate clauses.
- There are some seventy-five special words in these chapters which are not found in Paul's other writings. Instead of the word "gospel", here we have "mystery".
- There are none of Paul's customary personal greetings and no allusions to his past.
- The teaching has moved on from Paul's earlier emphasis on Israel, the cross and the return of Christ. Here we have the risen Christ, seated on the heavenly throne, presiding as the glorious head of his bride, the universal Church.

Adult education was important for Paul. We know from Acts 19:9-10 that he spent two years as a lecturer in the college of Tyrannus in Ephesus. Perhaps that's why this later letter has a more sophisticated feel to it.

The great doctrinal theme is the fullness of Christ offered to the Gentiles in the universal Church.

Chapter 1 honours the fantastic richness of the gifts we have received from the Father (1:3-6), Son (1:7-12) and Spirit (1:13-14).

The dignity of all the baptised is stressed in **chapter 2** – "you are no longer strangers and aliens, but you are citizens with the saints and also members of the household of God" (2:19).

Chapter 3 tells how the Gentiles are to be given "the news of the boundless riches of Christ" (3:8). One of the great New Testament prayers of praise follows:

"I bow my knees before the Father, from whom every family in heaven and on earth takes its name… I pray that you may have the power to comprehend, with all the saints, what is the breadth and length and height and depth, and to know the love of Christ that surpasses knowledge… Now to him who by the power at work within us is able to accomplish abundantly far more than all we can ask or imagine, to him be glory in the church and in Christ Jesus to all generations, for ever and ever. Amen." (3:14-21)

Ephesians has a strong ecumenical flavour and **chapter 4** offers a great call to unity: "There is one body and one Spirit… one Lord, one faith, one baptism, one God and Father of all" (4:4-6). The emphasis is not on juridical or hierarchical unity, but on a living or vital unity that binds everyone to the head, Jesus Christ.

Chapters 5 and 6 are a prompt to Christian ideals – pure and sober living, singing and chanting to the Lord, and everywhere giving thanks to God (5:20).

This section also contains one of the most controversial of Paul's teachings: "Just as the church is subject to Christ, so also wives ought to be, in everything, to their husbands " (5:24).

The whole context of the phrase is one of love. Any wifely subordination is modelled on the Church's loving response to the love that Christ gives his Church. In no way is this a call for the demeaning of wives. Paul's teaching elsewhere is quite clear: "There is no longer Jew or Greek, there is no longer slave or free, there is no longer male and female; for all of you are one in Christ Jesus" (Galatians 3:28).

Like the introduction to the letter, the personal conclusion seems to have done the rounds – possibly lifted from the end of Colossians (Colossians 4:7-8).

"Please, Miss, it wasn't me!" Did we ever say that when the teacher blamed us for something? Poor St Paul probably feels like this when people accuse him of giving women a really hard time in the early days of the Church! And yes, we do hear it read out to us: "Women should be silent in the churches. For they are not permitted to speak, but should be subordinate, as the law also says. If there is anything they desire to know, let them ask their husbands at home. For it is shameful for a woman to speak in church." Whoever first said that, it "wasn't" Paul!

Yes, the words appear in his first letter to the church in Corinth (14:33-36). But this letter is a response to two letters Paul himself has received about the Corinthian church. One of them is from a woman called Chloe. She is concerned about the way things are going in Paul's absence:

- Christian groups are hurling sectarian chants at one another (1:10 – 4:21);
- there is the scandal of incest (5:1-13);
- Christians are washing their dirty linen in public and are engaging in lawsuits against one another (6:1-11);
- and sexual promiscuity is going on all over the place (6:12-20).

These are *big* problems and Chloe needs the help of Paul's voice of authority. This woman is far from "silent" and is courageously speaking out in prophetic reform. Paul respects this and answers her letter as fully as he can in 1 Corinthians 1:10 – 6:20.

However, there is a second piece of correspondence, a "report" sent to Paul from certain menfolk. Paul's response runs from 7:1 to 15:58. The report has raised four main issues:

- sex – lifestyle matters of virginity, marriage and widowhood (7:1-40);
- the problems of conscience some people have in eating meat that has been offered to idols (8:1 – 11:1);
- public order when Christians meet for worship (11:2 – 14:40);
- and lastly the matter of personal resurrection from the dead (15:1-58).

It is in the area concerning public order that we find the words "women should be silent in the churches". But Paul is *quoting* what the men have said in their report to him! Paul often quotes things from other sources: "each of you says, 'I belong to Paul', or 'I belong to Apollos', or 'I belong to Cephas', or 'I belong to Christ'" (1:12); "All things are lawful" (6:12; 10:23); "how can some of you say there is no resurrection of the dead?" (15:12).

Paul does indeed want order and so he writes, "God is a God not of disorder but of peace" (14:33). But after quoting the men's report about women's silence he chides the men: "Or did

the word of God originate with you? Or are you the only ones it has reached?" (14:38). In this verse, the "you" is in the masculine in Paul's Greek. If Paul were rebuking the women, the Greek would have been obviously in the feminine.

Two other points can be noted:

- first, and importantly, Paul obviously approves of women praying and prophesying in church (11:5);
- second, it is quite unlike Paul to stress obedience to "the law", as in 14:34. To him normally "the power of sin is the law" (15:56). He has advocated freedom from the law (Galatians 3:24-25).

For Paul the bottom line was laid down in the result of everyone's commitment in baptism:

"As many of you as were baptized into Christ have clothed yourselves with Christ. There is no longer Jew or Greek, there is no longer slave or free, there is no longer male and female; for all of you are one in Christ Jesus." (Galatians 3:27-28)

Paul often mentions his female co-workers. On one occasion two women leaders in Philippi fell out with one another; so Paul wrote:

"I urge Euodia and I urge Syntyche to be of the same mind in the Lord. Yes, and I ask you also, my loyal companion, help these women, for they have struggled beside me in the work of the gospel, together with Clement and the rest of my co-workers, whose names are in the book of life." (Philippians 4:2-3)

These women are reckoned in the company of the great Clement, future bishop of Rome!

At the end of his letter to the Romans Paul mentions a whole group of female co-workers:

- Phoebe, a commissioned church officer (*diakonon*, a word used of men too in 1 Corinthians 3:5);
- Prisca and Aquila, a married couple where the probably more important woman Prisca is mentioned first! (See also Acts 18:1-3. 18-26);
- Mary, Tryphaena and Tryphosa, whom he calls "workers" like Paul himself (16:6. 12);
- and Andronicus and Junia, "prominent among the apostles" (16:7).

"Silent women"? It wasn't Paul!

The women
WOMEN WHO FOLLOWED JESUS

Someone has counted all the named characters of the Hebrew scriptures. It may not come as a surprise to learn that there are 1,426 named men and only 111 named women.

When we move to the New Testament the situation is greatly improved, but we still find several nameless women like "the daughter of Jairus", or the "bent woman", or the "woman in the city" who anointed the feet of Jesus.

Our high regard for the named apostles should not lead us to ignore those faithful and named women who followed Jesus right to the end, even when all the menfolk had fled. Luke can be our guide into this story:

"[Jesus] went on through cities and villages, proclaiming and bringing the good news of the kingdom of God. The twelve were with him, as well as some women who had been cured of evil spirits and infirmities: Mary, called Magdalene, from whom seven demons had gone out, and Joanna, the wife of Herod's steward Chuza, and Susanna, and many others, who provided for them out of their resources." (Luke 8:1-3)

At a time when sicknesses were considered the work of demons, Mary Magdalene was one of a group of women who had been healed by Jesus – "seven demons" could indicate a severe illness. They all followed him and supported him from their resources.

Joanna was perhaps particularly well off, since she was married to the king's steward. Emperors and kings had such a well-paid official who could be trusted to safeguard their financial interests.

It is important to sort out one or two misunderstandings about Mary Magdalene. Contrary to popular belief, she was not a prostitute. The woman of the city who wept and wet the feet of Jesus with her tears and anointed his feet in Luke 7:38 is unnamed by Luke. Since we do not know her name, we could identify this woman as the repentant woman. We should not call her Mary Magdalene.

Contrary to popular belief again, Mary Magdalene was not the sister of Lazarus. We remember the story of Jesus going to Bethany, near Jerusalem, where Martha did all the serving while a Mary sat at the feet of Jesus (Luke 10:38-42). This person we could call "Mary of Bethany". There is no evidence for identifying her with Mary Magdalene, who came from Galilee in the north.

Who, then, was Mary Magdalene? As we have seen, she was one of the first followers of Jesus who supported Jesus on his travels, providing resources together with other named women.

She followed Jesus to the very end, since the Gospels describe her at the crucifixion as watching, and waiting near the tomb to attend to the body (John 19:25; Matthew 27:56. 61). She was one of the first witnesses to the resurrection (Matthew 28:1-9; John 20:11-18). We could guess that she was in her early twenties, since normally a young person could speedily run the mile or so to the house where the disciples were gathered!

She has been called *Apostola Apostolorum*, the "apostle to the apostles" – although they didn't believe her womanly tale!

Clopas

When we come to considering the women at the cross, we find three women in Matthew, Mark and Luke, but Jesus' mother mentioned only in John. (See the table below.) Matthew, Mark and Luke have their three women present after the death of Jesus, and "at a distance". Luke alone says that male followers too were there, "at a distance" (Luke 23:49). In addition to the Galilean women, Luke also has women of Jerusalem present.

Matthew	Mark	Luke	John
27:56	15:40	24:10	19:25
1. Mary Magdalene	1. Mary Magdalene	1. Mary Magdalene	1. Mary Magdalene
2. Mary mother of James and Joseph (sons of Clopas?)	2. Mary mother of James ("the younger") and Joses (sons of Clopas?)	2. Mary mother of James (son of Clopas?)	2. Mary wife of Clopas, "his mother's sister" (sister-in-law?)
3. Mother of the sons of Zebedee (= James and John)	3. Salome	3. Joanna (wife of Chuza)	3. (The beloved disciple)
			4. Jesus' mother
Three women	Three named women	Three named women	Three women

100

All four Gospels have Mary Magdalene on the scene. Can the second named woman, "Mary the wife of Clopas", "Mary the mother of James" and "Mary the mother of James and Joseph (or Joses)", all be the same person? It depends on who Clopas was.

The second-century historian Hegesippus of Palestine tells us that Clopas was the brother of St Joseph. That would make him Jesus' uncle, and so his wife, Mary the wife of Clopas, would be Jesus' aunt Mary. Their children, Joseph (Joses = "Josie") and James (James "the younger"), would be cousins of Jesus – "brothers of the Lord". If you are following this family-tree business, then this Mary the wife of Clopas would be Our Lady's sister-in-law, related through Joseph. John's Gospel calls her simply "his mother's sister".

What we are seeing in all of this is the gathering of Jesus' closest women followers and relatives near the cross. Joanna, the wife of Chuza, is still there. John's Gospel tells us that a man, the beloved disciple, was also nearby. (The Greek word *para* does not mean "under" the cross. In fact there was a Roman decree after the death of Sejanus in AD 31, prohibiting relatives from getting too close to the executed person, though whether this was observed in far-off Jerusalem is not known.)

But the mother of Jesus and the beloved disciple are near enough for the dying Jesus to speak to them and link them even more closely. The model disciple and the mother move into a new family relationship.

Many people assume that the beloved disciple was John the Galilean fisherman, the son of Zebedee, although other claims have been made for him.

New Eve, new creation

Now here is a strange thing: Matthew tells us that the "mother of the sons of Zebedee" – the mother of James and John – was present. Was her name Salome, the name mentioned by Mark?

So it seems that, with John's own mother standing by, the dying Jesus commends John to Our Lady. Surely Jesus is not breaking up a family! Rather he is identifying his mother's role as the new Eve at this new creation. She is the mother of the whole new community, into which he now pours his Spirit. The infant Church is born from the cross.

There is an interesting tailpiece that Luke alone mentions. He tells us about the two disciples on the road to Emmaus (24:13-35). One of them is Cleopas. Is the other unnamed disciple his wife, Mary "the wife of Clopas"?

Clopas is an Aramaic name. In Greek it could be Cleopas. A man could respond to either name, just as Simeon and Simon are Aramaic and Greek names for the same person.

The risen Lord appears to them in the breaking of bread. We know that they rushed back there and then to the eleven and their companions and told their news, only to meet the risen Lord again and share with him – of all things – a fish supper (Luke 24:42)!

It's easy to be carried away when you're in love. Some of our devotional hymns tend to do this, asking Mary, for example, to "remind thy son that he has paid the price of our iniquity", as though Mary were more thoughtful than the crucified one (not to mention the awful image of a God who demands a price)!

So what do the Gospels say about Mary?

Mark: The earliest Gospel, Mark, seems to stress that discipleship must take priority over biological family ties.

In Mark 3:20-21 Jesus is too busy to find time to eat, and his family exclaim: "He has gone out of his mind." Later, when Jesus is surrounded by his disciples, his family, who are outside the group, reject him and Jesus comments: "Prophets are not without honour, except in their home town, and among their own kin, and in their own house" (6:4).

For Mark, it is the cross that is crucial for discipleship. There can be no family privileges without this. It may come as a surprise that Mark, like Matthew and Luke, does not indicate the presence of Mary at Golgotha.

Matthew: When we come to the Gospel of Matthew we find that family is important as well as discipleship. The revelation of salvation is first made in the annunciation not to Mary but to Joseph (1:18-25). He learns that Jesus is virginally conceived in Mary by the power of the Holy Spirit. This is a truly powerful indication of the role of Mary in God's plan of salvation.

Luke: Moving on to the Gospel of Luke, we find that revelation of Jesus as Son of God and Son of David is first made to Mary (1:26-38). She is the one who gladly receives the Good News. She is hailed by Elizabeth as "the mother of my Lord", and proclaims the great rebel song, the Magnificat (1:39-56). Further, Mary learns from Simeon that a sword of division will pierce her heart (2:35). She will learn that discipleship involves suffering. Her faith and understanding have to grow as she learns as a human mother

to let go of her son and understand him better.

Several times Luke tells us of Mary's struggles. She is "much perplexed" at the angel's greeting (1:29). When the shepherds tell Mary about their heavenly experience, Luke tells us that she "treasured all these words and pondered them in her heart" (2:19) – churning them over again and again inside her. When Simeon tells her that Jesus is to be a light for the Gentiles, Mary is "amazed at what was being said" (2:33). And when the boy Jesus tells his parents that he must be about his Father's business (or in his Father's house) they are "astonished" and simply do not understand; and "his mother treasured all these things in her heart" (2:48-51).

Later, when a woman exclaims: "Blessed is the womb that bore you and the breasts that nursed you!" Jesus corrects her and sees beyond Mary's biological motherhood – he says Mary is indeed blessed, but it is because she has heard God's word and kept it (11:27-29). Like the good seed, Mary hears the word of God and keeps it, and is praised by Jesus for this. But it hasn't been easy, and it takes time.

We could sum up Luke's Gospel portrait of Mary by saying that she is the first to accept God's word with her fiat, and the model disciple who listens and acts upon it.

In Luke's second volume, Acts, Mary carries on the witness of prayerful discipleship, with the women, the apostles and the family relatives in the upper room. Mary is at the heart of the new community (Acts 1:14).

John: If we had only the Gospel of John, we would never know the name of the mother of Jesus. For he refers to her simply, but dramatically, as "the mother of Jesus" or as "woman". This

woman appears in two scenes in John.

The first is at Cana (2:1-11). Jesus' mother puts a family request. The family members are there. They expect Jesus to live up to the family expectations. Jesus refutes this. He has to establish a priority of God's mission over any family expectations. Yet the scene is not negative. There is a rejection by Jesus at first, but Mary shows a willingness to listen to her son; and then Jesus goes ahead and transforms the situation. The symbolism of the great act must not be missed: the huge water pots for the Jewish purification ritual are replaced by the joyful wine of the new time of God's salvation! The symbolic and real role of the woman will become clearer as Jesus' mother becomes the new Eve at a new creation, when Jesus'"hour" comes to its climax on Golgotha.

This second scene takes place around the cross. Unlike in the other Gospels, Jesus is not alone here. Both his mother and the beloved disciple are standing there. Neither is named. Both acquire a new relationship and role as Jesus says with his dying breath: "Woman, here is your son… Here is your mother" (19:25-27). A new family relationship is created.

The disciple whom Jesus loved is now son of Mary and therefore brother of Jesus. Mary is not highlighted here as being Jesus' mother but rather as mother of the ideal disciple. She and the beloved disciple are foundational disciples of the new believing community. From the cross, Jesus breathes forth his Spirit upon the infant Church and utters the great victory cry: "It is finished" (19:30). He has completed the work given to him by the Father.

There is much to reflect upon in these four Gospel traditions.

Pope Paul VI, in his encyclical on devotion to Mary, *Marialis Cultus*, wrote about Marian devotion being rooted in scripture. However, he gave us not one but four guidelines – biblical, liturgical, ecumenical and anthropological. Anthropological? Yes!

Mary can be a spokeswoman for the poor and oppressed of society. The poorest of the poor are often women, women with children, abused and exploited by the rich – who are often men.

The prophetic role of the woman, expressed in the Magnificat, is highly relevant for us all today.

THE MAGNIFICAT

It was the German theologian Dietrich Bonhoeffer, killed by the Nazis, who in a sermon preached in 1933 described the Magnificat as "the oldest Advent hymn".

"The Song of Mary", he said, "has none of the sweet, nostalgic, or even playful tones of some of our Christmas carols. It is instead a hard, strong, inexorable song about collapsing thrones and humbling the lords of this world… These are the tones of the woman prophets of the Old Testament that now come to life in Mary's mouth."

We can read this hymn in chapter 1 of the Gospel of Luke. That's where Mary goes to visit her cousin Elizabeth.

In the song we find six very strong verbs: showing strength, scattering, filling up, pulling down, lifting up, sending away. In many ways it is a rebel song. It was even banned in Guatemala during the 1980s since it was deemed so subversive!

In Luke's Gospel, the hymn provides a noble preface to the programme that Jesus will proclaim during his ministry. He will say in his local synagogue, perhaps in the presence of his mother, that he was the person sent by God to bring good news to those who are poor and oppressed and to set prisoners free.

In the Beatitudes he will proclaim the greatness of God's favour for the poor, the hungry, the abused and persecuted remnants of society, burdened by Roman rule and male religious domination. Is Jesus reflecting his mother's influence during his upbringing?

This strong Galilean peasant woman would be acutely aware of the injustices around her; the song that Luke puts on her lips seems to be modelled on the Maccabean war hymns we find in the Dead Sea Scrolls.

It also reflects the song of Hannah (1 Samuel 2:1-10), who sings,

"My heart exults in the Lord;
my strength is exalted in my God…
The bows of the mighty are broken,
but the feeble gird on strength.
Those who were full have hired themselves
out for bread,
but those who were hungry are fat with spoil."

Mary's hymn consists of two great blocks of poetry. The first celebrates the greatness of the saviour God. It recalls Mary's namesake, the Old Testament woman of strength Miriam, sister of Moses, with her tambourine and her singing and dancing in praise of the Lord (Exodus 15:1-21).

While the first section of the Magnificat has been described as "raising a toast" to God, the second section proclaims how God brings justice to those who are weak by turning the power structures upside down.

We hear frequently about Mary's "Yes" – "let it be". This, of course, is rightly proclaimed. It is a positive and responsible commitment to the invitation of a gracious Lord at the annunciation.

But in the Magnificat she also is a proponent of "No!" wherever injustice is around:

- No to the mighty! They need to be toppled from their power structures.
- No to those who cause starvation! The hungry poor must be fed.
- No to those who deny the dignity of every person, born or unborn! Human dignity needs to be affirmed among all, whatever their colour, gender, creed or social standing; and especially those who live in poverty.

The Redemptorist biblical scholar Fr Denis McBride writes about Mary voicing her Magnificat from "a Cinderella people" – a lovely phrase, full of hope:

"The proud are toppled from their precious pedestals; the mighty find themselves unemployed; the little people are unimportant no more; the hungry are attended to at last; the rich are solemnly awarded nothing. The Magnificat praises the revolution of God."

As part of the prayer of the Church, the Magnificat is proclaimed each day during Evening Prayer. In music, it is sung in many forms, from Bach to the more modest local compositions, including a popular setting to the tune "Amazing Grace".

It is quite remarkable that the Magnificat, the hymn of Miriam of Nazareth, has found its way into the grass-roots piety of today's pilgrim people as we celebrate the amazing grace of God our saviour who has done great things for us.

Our earliest Advent hymn still looks for our gracious response.

▍MARY OR MIRIAM?

People sometimes wonder why we know the mother of Jesus as "Mary" while to her companions in Nazareth she would be called "Miriam".

The Greek translation of the name is "Maria", which we carry over in our English translations of the New Testament. But when the Old Testament Hebrew language or the Aramaic of the time was used, then the same name appeared as "Miriam".

Scholars give various meanings to the name: "the Lord's woman"; "the fat one" (being fat was a sign of great beauty in that culture!); and "rebel". So we might peer behind the chinks of tradition and describe Mary as "God's beautiful rebel".

▍MAGNIFICAT

"My soul magnifies the Lord,
and my spirit rejoices in God my Saviour,
for he has looked with favour on the lowliness of his servant.
Surely, from now on all generations will call me blessed;
for the Mighty One has done great things for me,
and holy is his name.
His mercy is for those who fear him
from generation to generation.
He has shown strength with his arm;
he has scattered the proud in the thoughts of their hearts.
He has brought down the powerful from their thrones,
and lifted up the lowly;
he has filled the hungry with good things,
and sent the rich away empty.
He has helped his servant Israel,
in remembrance of his mercy,
according to the promise he made to our ancestors,
to Abraham and to his descendants for ever."
(Luke 1:46-55)

THREE WOMEN WHO PERSIST

There are three unnamed women in Mark's Gospel who are honoured by Jesus.

Woman One

There is the woman with the haemorrhage in Mark 5:25-34. Because she had been bleeding for twelve years she was legally barred from mingling with ordinary people. The book of Leviticus (15:25) had laid down the regulations. She was an "untouchable" in every sense. And it was unthinkable that a woman in her condition would deliberately reach out and touch someone else. But she sees Jesus making his way to the house of Jairus to heal his little girl, and secretly and quietly takes the initiative, breaks with taboos, puts her faith in the healer. She reaches out and touches him, in spite of thus making him ritually unclean in the eyes of the Law.

Normally in Mark it is the man Jesus who takes the initiative where healing is required. This woman has stepped out of the conventions of her culture. Yet she feels she must now slip away back into the background from which she came. Jesus will have none of that. So, in spite of her anxiety, she publicly proclaims "the whole truth" about Jesus. Jesus greets her as "Daughter", saying to her: "your faith has made you well; go in peace, and be healed of your disease". She has taken the initiative, made a bold decision for herself. She has come out of hiding, and now she gives public witness to Jesus. He looks at her, affirms her dignity, and she is healed in more ways than one. Jesus sees her as an example of taking the initiative and putting faith into action.

Woman Two

There is the second unnamed woman, found in Mark 14:3-9. In Bethany she interrupts the meal with all the male guests at the table of Simon (who had a virulent skin disease, by the way). This woman is not to be confused with Mary Magdalene or with Mary of Bethany, the sister of Martha and Lazarus. She comes in with an expensive jar of perfumed ointment. She breaks it open (to pour it abundantly and speedily) and spreads it over the head of Jesus.

The male guests are angry with her. Her wasteful extravagance annoys them. The men's sharp criticism does not deter her. She has the insight to see that Jesus will suffer and she has the touching sensitivity to anoint (literally "to christen") him in prophetic anticipation of his burial. Jesus sees her as a prophet and declares that, wherever the Gospel will be proclaimed, this unnamed woman will be remembered for this.

Woman Three

The third unnamed woman in Mark (7:25-30) is a foreigner, a woman from Syria who followed after Jesus when he went into a house in non-Jewish Tyre "and did not want anyone to know he was there". What? Jesus goes into a Gentile house and wants to keep this a dark secret? His vocation was to the House of Israel, so he thought!

Then this Gentile woman somehow gets to him. A Gentile woman, without a man to speak for her, requests help for her daughter. Her boldness puts Jesus on the spot. She challenges him to widen his horizons. But he has come for the lost sheep of the House of Israel, not for "the dogs". The wit and determination of this northern woman come to the fore: "even the dogs under the table eat the children's crumbs", she argues. Eager, playful puppies under the children's table form quite a contrast to dozy sheep that have wandered from their God-given pasture! Jesus must have laughed. The lone mum certainly gets her way, and the daughter is healed. From now on in Mark, Jesus reaches out to Gentiles, perhaps as a result of her "dogged" persistence!

In Mark's three stories about unnamed women we have Jesus respecting the unexpected, valuing those who break through the social and religious barriers that keep people down.

The woman with blood problems has her dignity affirmed by Jesus. Today he welcomes all who feel cut off by the misunderstandings surrounding HIV and blood-borne viruses such as hepatitis C. Furthermore, Jesus is not one to turn away people who feel excluded by cultural conventions surrounding some of our religious rituals.

The prophetic woman who anointed Jesus sees, perhaps through her own womanly experience, a positive and saving value hidden in the violence of the personal suffering that lies ahead for Jesus.

Lastly, the foreign mother, who seems to have shaped the outreach of Jesus to non-Jews, may give us further reason today to see God's love alive in people beyond our own little flock.

All of us today, men as well as women, can surely explore these stories to find enrichment for developing a responsible spirituality.

When we first learned to make the sign of the cross we probably had some idea of what we meant by "the Father" and "the Son". But this "Holy Spirit" bit wasn't so easy to grasp.

Maybe we can be encouraged by the words of Jesus in John 3:8. He tells us that we really cannot "grasp" God:

"The wind [or Spirit] blows where it chooses, and you hear the sound of it, but you do not know where it comes from or where it goes."

In the Bible God's Spirit is described as a powerful wind, the breath of life, the energy of fire, the seal of God on the perfect work of Christ, and as God's special gift to us. God's Spirit is all over the place in the Bible.

The word for "spirit" in the Aramaic language that Jesus probably spoke is *rucha*, and it is a feminine word. So too is the word for "spirit" in the liturgical Hebrew language: here it is *ruach*.

But while the New Testament Greek word for "spirit" (*pneuma*) is neutral in gender, it nevertheless gets masculine adjectives joined to it in John's Gospel:

"When the Spirit of truth comes, he will guide you into all the truth; for he will not speak on his own, but will speak whatever he hears, and he will declare to you the things that are to come. He will glorify me, because he will take what is mine and declare it to you." (John 16:13-15; also 15:26; 16:8)

So it's not quite biblical to argue, as some do, that the Holy Spirit is feminine. God is obviously more than masculine or feminine.

The Spirit prepares for Jesus

It is fascinating to see how God gradually reveals the Spirit throughout the Bible. At the start of Genesis, it was God's Spirit that moved over the chaos to bring about an orderly creation (Genesis 1:1-2). Then God breathed ("spirited") the breath of life into the dust to create a living being (*nephesh* in Hebrew), a human who was animated by God's gift of the breath of life (2:7).

We learn too that God's Spirit consecrated kings and priests and energised the prophets (1 Samuel 16:13; 2 Chronicles 24:20; Ezekiel 11:24; Isaiah 61:1).

In due course, God's Spirit hovered over the Virgin Mary at the incarnation (Matthew 1:18; Luke 1:35) and "the Word became flesh and lived among us" (John 1:14).

The Spirit comes through Jesus

Luke has been described as the evangelist of the Spirit. His Gospel mentions the Holy Spirit some thirteen times – contrast Mark's four and Matthew's five references – and Luke's second volume, the Acts of the Apostles, has some thirty-nine references to the Holy Spirit. But the Gospel of John has its own profound perspectives on Jesus and the Spirit.

- Firstly, the evangelist has the Baptist saying:

"I saw the Spirit descending from heaven like a dove, and it remained on him. I myself did not know him, but the one who sent me to baptise with water said to me, 'He on whom you see the Spirit descend and remain is the one who baptises with the Holy Spirit.' And I myself have seen and have testified that this is the Son of God." (John 1:32-34)

God's Spirit remains in Jesus.

- Secondly, Jesus promises that he will pour out this Spirit at the appropriate time, when he will be "lifted up", exalted on the cross (John 7:39).
- Then, as Jesus dies on the cross, the evangelist boldly states that Jesus bowed his head and "gave up his spirit"… gave it to the new creation, the infant Church near the cross, to the "woman", the new Eve, and to the beloved disciple, the ideal follower, beside her (John 19:25-30).
- Finally, on Easter night, the risen Jesus breathes on the chaos of the gathered disciples:

"When it was evening on that day, the first day of the week, and the doors of the house where the disciples had met were locked for fear of the Jews, Jesus came and stood among them and said, 'Peace be with you.' After he said this, he showed them his hands and his side. Then the disciples rejoiced when they saw the Lord. Jesus said to them again, 'Peace be with you. As the Father has sent me, so I send you.' When he had said this, he breathed on them and said to them, 'Receive the Holy Spirit.'" (John 20:19-22)

The Spirit is gifted to the gathered community.

The Spirit in our lives

The biblical story of God's energising Spirit goes on, with the gift being poured out to all nations through Pentecost, and with Paul's great teaching on the fruits of the Spirit: "the fruit of the Spirit is love, joy, peace, patience, kindness, generosity, faithfulness, gentleness, and self-control" (Galatians 5:22-23).

These fruits should arise in our lives from the gifts of the Spirit, just as the fruits of a tree arise from its roots.

The gifts of the Spirit are listed in the Church's ritual of confirmation. This beautiful prayer, which has its roots in words of the prophet Isaiah (11:1-2), is said by the bishop as he extends his hands over those who are being confirmed:

"All-powerful God, Father of our Lord Jesus Christ,
by water and the Holy Spirit
you freed your sons and daughters from sin
and gave them new life.
Send your Holy Spirit upon them
to be their helper and guide.
Give them the spirit of wisdom and
understanding,
the spirit of right judgement and courage,
the spirit of knowledge and reverence.
Fill them with the spirit of wonder and awe in
your presence.
We ask this through Christ our Lord.
Amen."

GIFTS OF THE SPIRIT

Awe and wonder: "In the beginning when God created the heavens and the earth, the earth was a formless void and darkness covered the face of the deep, while a wind from God swept over the face of the waters. Then God said, 'Let there be light'; and there was light." (Genesis 1:1-3)

Spirit of the living God, may your gift of awe and wonder lead us to the fruit of self-control as we respect all of creation and protect life in all its stages.

Reverence: "The Lord God formed man from the dust of the ground, and breathed into his nostrils the breath of life; and the man became a living being." (Genesis 2:7)

Spirit of the living God, may your gift of reverence lead us to the fruit of gentleness as we respectfully treat ourselves and one another as temples of the Holy Spirit.

Wisdom: "God gave Solomon very great wisdom, discernment, and breadth of understanding… Solomon's wisdom surpassed the wisdom of all the people of the east, and all the wisdom of Egypt." (1 Kings 4:29-30)

Spirit of the living God, may your wisdom be with us and our leaders, and guide us into true joy and peace.

Knowledge: "The angel said to her, 'The Holy Spirit will come upon you, and the power of the Most High will overshadow you; therefore the child to be born will be holy; he will be called Son of God'… Then Mary said, 'Here am I, the servant of the Lord; let it be with me according to your word.'" (Luke 1:35-38)

Spirit of the living God, may we seek to know more clearly your will and use your gift of knowledge to produce fruits of greater trustfulness in you and one another.

Right judgement: "Then Jesus, filled with the power of the Spirit, returned to Galilee, and a report about him spread through all the surrounding country…

When he came to Nazareth, where he had been brought up, he went to the synagogue on the sabbath day, as was his custom. He stood up to read, and the scroll of the prophet Isaiah was given to him. He unrolled the scroll and found the place where it was written: 'The Spirit of the Lord is upon me, because he has anointed me to bring good news to the poor.'" (Luke 4:14-18)

Spirit of the living God, may we use your gift of right judgement with patience, as we endeavour to read the signs of the times and to bring good news to those who are poor – whether mentally, spiritually, economically or physically poor.

Understanding: "When Jesus saw his mother and the disciple whom he loved standing beside her, he said to his mother, 'Woman, here is your son.' Then he said to the disciple, 'Here is your mother'… When Jesus had received the wine, he said, 'It is finished.' Then he bowed his head and gave up his spirit." (John 19:26-30)

Spirit of the living God, breathed out from the cross onto the infant Church beneath, may we use your gift of understanding to build up around us in practical ways a community that bears and shares the fruits of love.

Courage: "When the day of Pentecost had come, they were all together in one place. And suddenly from heaven there came a sound like the rush of a violent wind, and it filled the entire house where they were sitting. Divided tongues, as of fire, appeared among them, and a tongue rested on each of them. All of them were filled with the Holy Spirit and began to speak in other languages, as the Spirit gave them ability." (Acts 2:1-4)

Spirit of the living God, may we use your gift of courage to produce fruits of goodness and kindness, as we bear witness to our faith in word and in action, in our homes and families as well as in the work of evangelisation to the very ends of the earth.

The Christian feast of Pentecost was a long time in coming. Just as Luke is the only one to mention the ascension, so too is he alone in speaking of a Pentecost event.

What did the old Jewish feast of Pentecost mean for Jesus as a boy? It had probably several meanings. It was a feast day, with a word that meant "fiftieth", one more than seven times seven, a strong hint at completeness. In practice it was linked with the feast of Passover:

"[After Passover] you shall count off seven weeks; they shall be complete. You shall count until the day after the seventh sabbath, fifty days; then you shall present an offering of new grain to the Lord." (Leviticus 23:15-16)

So probably it was originally a feast of thanksgiving to celebrate the harvesting of wheat. It had at least two aspects: firstly, at the family level, it became the occasion for a celebratory family meal, a special time of thanksgiving for the gift of abundant food. We can read how Tobit says,

"During the reign of Esar-haddon I returned home, and my wife Anna and my son Tobias were restored to me. At our festival of Pentecost, which is the sacred festival of weeks, a good dinner was prepared for me and I reclined to eat. When the table was set for me and an abundance of food placed before me, I said to my son Tobias, 'Go, my child, and bring whatever poor person you may find of our people among the exiles in Nineveh, who is wholeheartedly mindful of God, and he shall eat together with me. I will wait for you, until you come back.'" (Tobit 2:1-2)

Secondly, on the public scene, it developed into a time for pilgrimage to the Temple in Jerusalem, an occasion to thank God openly for the gift of love sealed in the covenant (2 Maccabees 12:30-31). Later Judaism would have witnessed the destruction of the Temple by the Romans in AD 70, and so, instead of a pilgrimage feast, they would use the feast to celebrate the giving of Law to them through Moses on Mount Sinai.

When we come to read John's Gospel, we learn that it was on the evening of Easter, not Pentecost, that Jesus appeared, and there and then imparted the Spirit to the disciples (John 20:22). Like Mark and Matthew, John does not mention Pentecost as having any special significance. Only Luke gives us the deeper meaning of the traditional Jewish feast of Pentecost in Acts 2. But he does so using the powerful symbols of tongues of fire and gale-force winds; the Spirit is blowing now like a gale-force wind! The fear-filled silence of the apostles gives way to outspoken words of courage and to deeds that display the variety of gifts but always the same Spirit. Tongues are loosened and the many babbling, confusing languages of the old Tower of Babel are wonderfully *con*-fused, brought together, to receive the fire and light of God's powerful saving and transforming love in action.

This outpouring of the Spirit has been a long time in coming

In Genesis the Spirit moved over the chaos of the waters and what was the result? Light! (Genesis 1:3).
Come, Holy Spirit, come to the chaos of our experience today and bring your light for our voyages.

The Spirit came and imparted God's authority to Joshua when Moses formally laid hands on him and consecrated him for leadership (Deuteronomy 34:9).
Come, Holy Spirit, guide the leaders you have empowered for service among us by the laying on of hands.

The Spirit of artistic creativity was given to Bezalel when God "filled him with divine spirit, with skill, intelligence, and knowledge in every kind of craft, to devise artistic designs, to work in gold, silver, and bronze, in cutting stones for setting, and in carving wood, in every kind of craft. And he has inspired him to teach… with skill to do every kind of work done by an artisan or by a designer or by an embroiderer in blue, purple, and crimson yarns, and in fine linen, or by a weaver – by any sort of artisan or skilled designer" (Exodus 35:31-35).
Come, Holy Spirit, continue to inspire our artists, musicians, embroiderers, architects and teachers, so that the ongoing beauty of your creation may continue to be opened up to us for our responsible enjoyment in your service.

The Spirit came upon kings like David: "Samuel took the horn of oil, and anointed him in the presence of his brothers; and the spirit of the Lord came mightily upon David from that day forward" (1 Samuel 16:13).
Come, Holy Spirit, truly enlighten our political and religious leaders in their work of service.

The Spirit filled prophets, like Isaiah, who spoke of a successor to David: "A shoot shall come out from the stock of Jesse, and a branch shall grow out of his roots. The spirit of the Lord shall rest on him, the spirit of wisdom and understanding, the spirit of counsel and might, the spirit of knowledge and the fear of the Lord" (Isaiah 11:1-2). The prophet Ezekiel dreamt of a great future when the Spirit would re-energise the dry bones of God's community (Ezekiel 37:1-14).
Come, Holy Spirit, give renewed energy to your prophets today so that they may speak out powerfully to our Church and nation.

Finally, we remember how the Spirit overshadowed the Virgin Mary at Nazareth (Luke 1:35) and worked through Jesus as he announced his manifesto in Nazareth: "The Spirit of the Lord is upon me, because he has anointed me to bring good news to the poor. He has sent me to proclaim release to the captives and recovery of sight to the blind, to let the oppressed go free, to proclaim the year of the Lord's favour" (Luke 4:18-19).
Come, Holy Spirit, strengthen us too to be good news to the poor, to those who are blind and enslaved today, beginning with ourselves.

When we realise that the Bible mentions the Spirit in various ways over five hundred times (with two hundred of these in the Old Testament), it becomes clear how much God has desired to share the living Spirit with us. The theme word for our still ongoing Pentecost is surely "enthusiasm", a word that literally means "God-is-in". Can we match God's enthusiasm with our enthusiasm?

Come, Holy Spirit, fill the hearts of your faithful and renew the face of the earth.

"Paraclete" is one of those strange words we can just consider as a technical "Gospel word" that we read and then pass on without reflecting too much on its meaning. If we do dig deeper, then we can come to realise that each one of us could be a paraclete (with a small "p") to those around us. A paraclete is someone who responds to your need and stands beside you, or pleads for you like a defence lawyer, calling out on your behalf. A mother or father can be a paraclete for a child who needs help or comfort. A big brother or sister can be a paraclete for a bullied youngster. A justice worker can be a paraclete for those who are oppressed.

The word "paraclete" has two bits to it and comes from two Greek words: *para*, meaning alongside; and *kletos*, from *kalein*, to call out. A paraclete is someone who calls out on your behalf, and defends, supports and comforts you.

Some English translations of the Bible use the word "Advocate" instead of Paraclete. This means the same thing but uses the Latin roots *ad* (towards) and *vocatus* (called); again it means someone who is called towards us and who calls others to support us… and to support the truth of Jesus: "When the Advocate comes, whom I will send to you from the Father, the Spirit of truth who comes from the Father, he will testify on my behalf" (John 15:26).

The "Paraclete" (with a capital "P") is the one whom Jesus promises to send from the Father. While Jesus himself is a defender of his disciples, in his farewell sermon, at the Last Supper, he says, "I will not leave you orphaned" (or "comfortless" in some translations of John 14:18).

He promises to leave with them *another* paraclete: "If you love me, you will keep my commandments. And I will ask the Father, and he will give you another Advocate [or Paraclete], to be with you for ever" (John 14:15-16). The Greek for "another" here is *allos*, meaning "of the same sort", not *heteros* which would mean a "different kind".

This Paraclete will be our ongoing support and teacher after Jesus' ascension: "The Advocate [or Paraclete], the Holy Spirit, whom the Father will send in my name, will teach you everything, and remind you of all that I have said to you" (John 14:26). This Paraclete on the one hand condemns the false teaching which is "the sin of the world", namely disbelief in Jesus, and on the other hand continues to strengthen and teach the Church, in this way preserving us in the truth, uniting us and fostering holiness in us.

This teacher is also our comforter: "because I have said these things to you, sorrow has filled your hearts. Nevertheless, I tell you the truth: it is to your advantage that I go away, for if I do not go away, the Advocate [or Paraclete] will not come to you; but if I go, I will send him to you" (John 16:6-7).

It is wonderful to remind ourselves that, even though we are sinners, we have someone who will plead our cause for us. This is truly amazing, that the Paraclete is on the side of sinners, getting into the witness box and arguing in our defence!

So there is a purpose to the exaltation of Jesus on and through the cross: it is to send the promised Paraclete, who still comes alongside us to provide guidance, consolation and support throughout life's journey. And we, in our own day-to-day living, are most certainly called to be alongside others, to be ourselves paracletes to our brothers and sisters who are in need of support, comfort and sound teaching.

APOCALYPSE NOW!

The last book in the Bible, the Apocalypse or book of Revelation, is so strange! Blood is used to wash white; there are seven mysterious seals to be opened, seven trumpets to be blown, four coloured horses, a great heavenly war and a scarlet woman... all very odd for us today.

Yet it is in the Bible. It must be important. It must have made sense to someone. Those around it at the beginning understood very well what it was all about. They were undergoing fierce persecution and they needed every encouragement they could get. This is a book of encouragement, but it had to be written in secret code to safeguard its audience. Those not "in the know" would get bored with it and give up reading it – like many of us, perhaps? For modern Christians it is at least uncomfortable. How can we get into it?

Well, to begin with, it is all a bit messy: scholars tell us that it was written over a period of at least thirty years and that various writers inserted their own bits from time to time. Frequent interpolations don't make for smooth reading! No one knows just who was involved in the writing. It starts with "I, John, your brother, who share with you in Jesus the persecution...", but scholars tell us that this is neither the John of the Fourth Gospel nor the writer of the letters of John. The writer tells us that some of it at least was written on the Roman prison island of Patmos (1:9). The final compilation emerged around the mid 90s in Asia Minor in the Roman province of what we now call Turkey.

The message of the book is clear: Christ has conquered, so hang on in there and all will be well!

■ A MAP OF THE BOOK

The structure of the book may help us to get our bearings. It has six parts.

1. An introduction or prologue: 1:1-3

2. A set of letters to seven churches of Asia Minor: 1:4 – 3:22

3. Visions of the heavenly court:
   The one enthroned and the Lamb: 4:1 – 5:14
   The seven seals of secrecy: 6:1 – 8:1
   The seven heralding trumpets: 8:2 – 11:19

4. Visions of the struggle:
   The dragon, the beast and the Lamb: 12:1 – 14:20
   Seven plagues and seven bowls: 15:1 –16:21

5. Judgement of Babylon (i.e. Rome): 17:1 –19:10
   The victory of Christ and end of history: 19:11 – 22:5

6. Conclusion and final prayer: 22:6-21

The seven letters

In our churches today we are quite accustomed to receiving pastoral circular letters. We find seven of these in the Apocalypse.

The text of the seven letters can be found in 2:1 – 3:22. They are delivered along the postman's route going in turn to Ephesus, Smyrna, Pergamum, Thyatira, Sardis, Philadelphia and Laodicea.

Each letter is about Christ and includes:

- a single description of Christ relevant to the city addressed;
- a description of that church's special characteristics;
- Christ's warning or encouragement;
- Christ's promise of hope.

Let's see how each community is topically addressed.
Ephesus is famous for its Greek goddess Artemis (known as Diana in Rome), and its fertility and luscious vegetation. So in 2:7 the writer says that it is Christ who will re-enter Eden and give out the once-banned fruit!

Smyrna was abandoned and died into decay in 600 BC but came to life when rebuilt around 300 BC. It promoted the cult of Cybele, the goddess of nature, who died and rose again. So the church in Smyrna is told to remember that Christ is the one who really died and rose to life. Moreover, Smyrna had a circular road of gold, separating the rich from the poor; from a distance this looked like a crown on a hill. The author says that Smyrna's athletes who won got only a crown of flowers, not a crown of life; but "Be faithful", says the Lord, "and I will give you the crown of life" (2:10).

Pergamum was the location of the regional court; it boasted the Roman *ius gladii*, or sword of justice. The writer sees Christ as the one who wields the two-edged sword of judgement. The citizens of Pergamum used to wear an armband inscribed with a lucky charm. Sometimes the charm was a simple stone with the name of a god inscribed on it. While the law courts used a black stone for condemnation, the writer speaks of a "white stone" with "a new name" that would identify the wearer with the victory of Christ (2:17).

Thyatira had a temple to Apollo, a god who was associated with the sun; but the writer says it is really Christ's eyes and feet that blaze and shine out like the sun.

Sardis had a famous cemetery with one hundred burial mounds. Our writer admonishes the church there, telling them that their church is as dead as the people in that burial ground. Sardis was lazy: carelessly it had fallen to the armies of Cyrus and Antiochus. The writer scolds the church there for its sleepy self-sufficiency: "If you do not wake up, I will come like a thief" (3:3). Sardis had its tax scrolls and its book of citizenship. The writer speaks of the really important book, the book of life.

Philadelphia was the key and gateway to eastern Asia Minor. It was plagued by earthquakes, so that many residents moved out and stayed in the surrounding villages. In God's temple Christians must remain solid and not run off. The city had received a new name: it had at one time been renamed New Caesarea. Similarly a heavenly Jerusalem will reign for the thousand-year reign of Christ; a new Jerusalem will be revealed after the old heaven and earth pass away.

Laodicea was famous for its banking, textile industry and learning. Its medical school had a famous eye salve. Its church should buy this ointment so that it could really see Christ! "You say, 'I am rich, I have prospered, and I need nothing.' You do not realize that you are wretched, pitiable, poor, blind, and naked. Therefore I counsel you to buy from me gold refined by fire so that you may be rich; and white robes to clothe you and to keep the shame of your nakedness from being seen; and salve to anoint your eyes so that you may see" (3:17-18). Laodicea was also famous for the glossy black fabric it produced (so the writer talks of white, not black, garments).

The letters are all designed to give warnings on morality, complacency and the need for perseverance in face of the imminent persecution.

In summary, the challenges are:

- Ephesus: Christ is present in power among his churches.
- Smyrna: Listen to the Spirit with courage.
- Pergamum: Tolerance does not mean complacency.
- Thyatira: Challenge those who compromise.
- Sardis: Watch complacency and sleepy self-satisfaction.
- Philadelphia: I am coming soon!
- Laodicea: Because you are lukewarm I will spit you out of my mouth!

A change of tone

After these seven letters, the writer moves on to give us a number of strange visions, which may seem threatening to us. These are all written in the magnificent language of the Apocalypse. This is a special literary form. It is a way of writing that uses hidden symbols to convey the message of encouragement in times of crisis. Symbols? Read on!